The Faith of Queen Elizabeth pulls back the royal curtain to reveal a compassionate heart dedicated to serving the King of Kings. Shared through the eyes of a gifted storyteller, this book will inspire you.

ROMA DOWNEY, actress, producer, and
New York Times bestselling author

How I love this book! If you thought you knew all there was to know about one of the most recognizable women in the world, *The Faith of Queen Elizabeth* will surprise you and leave you in tears of gratitude that such a monarch exists.

JANE KIRKPATRICK, award-winning
author of *One More River to Cross*

The faith of Her Majesty the Queen is the diamond in the crown: forged under extreme pressure, a "beacon of inspiration" the world over, reflecting the light of the Lord she serves. Delffs's book foregrounds this faith with fluency and respect: an absorbing read.

RIGHT REVEREND DR. JILL DUFF, bishop of Lancaster

This book is a wonderful tribute to the life of Queen Elizabeth II and to her devotion to the people of the UK, the Commonwealth, and the Church of England. It describes her clear and authentic Christian faith that has inspired me and many others in following Jesus's example.

ANDREW R. PRATT, bishop of Blackburn's interfaith advisor

I am grateful to Dudley Delffs for this much-needed record of a remarkable woman of faith. Queen Elizabeth is pivotal in the history of Britain and the world, and this book is a fitting tribute to her. It is well researched, perceptively observed, and compellingly written.

STEVE BELL, author and speaker

This book provides exceptional insight on the faith of Queen Elizabeth II, who has demonstrated this virtue exceptionally, not only in the UK but also across the Commonwealth and globally. In doing so, Her Majesty has shown humility and respect by reaching out to people from all walks of life regardless of their race, colour, creed, or faith.

GULAB SINGH, Member of the British Empire,
Deputy Lieutenant

The Faith of Queen Elizabeth interweaves brilliantly the examples of the total dedication and commitment of our Queen, founded on her Christian beliefs and values. As a British national and an East African Indian Hindu woman, I stand witness to our Queen living out the main tenets and values reflected in the text of the Bhagavad Gita: duty, action, and renunciation. These are amply depicted by our Queen's commitment to the benefit of all the people of the UK and the Commonwealth, whom she serves with selflessness, love, and steadfastness.

MRS. CHARU AINSCOUGH, Order of the
British Empire, Justice of the Peace

The Faith of Queen Elizabeth reveals more than just this famous leader's public service for six decades—it points directly to her passionate commitment to Jesus Christ. Drawing on historical archives, royal biographies, and personal interviews, Dudley Delffs paints a vivid portrait of a believer answering God's call on her life and trusting him through every public triumph and personal trial. This book brings history alive in the best way, inspiring us through Queen Elizabeth's example to follow the King of Kings.

CRAIG GROESCHEL, pastor of Life.Church,
New York Times bestselling author

Delffs shows why Queen Elizabeth II is so admired, even by those who are skeptical of the monarchy itself. He argues that the Queen's deep and personal Christian faith accounts for her steadfast commitment to her role as Head of the Church and State in over six decades of duties and trials—including those of her own family. In what approaches a biography of the Queen (Anglophiles will quickly warm up to Delffs's love for all things British, not to mention his engaging style), he shows us the human Elizabeth beneath the royal trappings.

DR. WILLIAM KLEIN, professor of New Testament at Denver
Seminary, author of *Introduction to Biblical Interpretation*

Dudley Delffs has written an accessible, lively overview of Her Majesty's lifetime of achievements and challenges. Excellent research and knowledge of contemporary culture meld with personal anecdotes to reveal the Queen's deepest commitments to her family, nation, and the international community.

DR. PHYLLIS KLEIN, spiritual director and British literature specialist

The FAITH of QUEEN ELIZABETH

THE POISE, GRACE, AND QUIET STRENGTH BEHIND THE CROWN

DUDLEY DELFFS

ZONDERVAN

The Faith of Queen Elizabeth
Copyright © 2019 by Dudley Delffs

Requests for information should be addressed to:
Zondervan, *3900 Sparks Dr. SE, Grand Rapids, Michigan 49546*

Zondervan titles may be purchased in bulk for educational, business, fund-raising, or promotional use. For information, please email SpecialMarkets@Zondervan.com.

ISBN 978-0-310-35697-4 (hardcover)

ISBN 978-0-310-35887-9 (international trade paper edition)

ISBN 978-0-310-35699-8 (audio)

ISBN 978-0-310-35698-1 (ebook)

Cover photo: PA Images/Alamy Stock Photo
Interior design: Kait Lamphere

Printed in the United States of America

19 20 21 22 23 24 25 /LSC/ 15 14 13 12 11 10 9 8 7 6 5 4 3 2 1

To Norma Delffs,
my own Queen Mother

CONTENTS

Therefore I am sure that this, my Coronation, is not
the symbol of a power and a splendor that are gone
but a declaration of our hopes for the future, and
for the years I may, by God's Grace and Mercy,
be given to reign and serve you as your Queen.

—Coronation Day address,
1953

chapter one

DUTY *and* DESIRE

ANSWERING THE CALL TO SERVE

*I*n many ways, it was a typical weekday in North London. The early December sky held the dull sheen of pewter and the moist scent of an afternoon shower. Office workers with coffee in hand or a takeaway lunch rushed back to their cubicles. Locals carrying umbrellas stopped to chat on sidewalks outside the shops. Pensioners and new moms with strollers sauntered toward Barnard Park or King Square Gardens. The usual number of tourists, perhaps lost or looking for Angel tube station or Caledonian Road, wandered about, pausing for the occasional selfie.

On a backstreet in a typically quiet neighborhood, however, a small crowd lined the curb near St. Mary's Islington, a steepled brick parish church dating to the eleventh century. A service of some kind was clearly about to begin, as smartly dressed couples and families mingled among enormous pillars before pouring through double doors. Within a few minutes, only a dozen or so formally dressed men and women, along with a handful of clergy, lingered outside the main entrance. Then the crowd erupted as a police car turned on to the block, followed by a black SUV and another sleek dark vehicle bearing a small pennant on top.

Stopping directly in front of the church, the claret-red and black car, known as the Bentley State Limousine, discharged its only passenger as a dark-suited attendant opened the vehicle's rear door. The smiling woman who emerged electrified the crowd filling the sidewalk only a few feet away as a royal guard in full dress uniform greeted her with a small nod and a proper handshake. Dressed in a bright fuchsia coat over a pink and red dress with a matching pink hat adorned with red feathers, the woman stepped up onto the open-air portico to be welcomed by the attendant clergy. On her left arm hung an iconic black Launer handbag.

Her Majesty Queen Elizabeth II had arrived.

Compared with most official royal arrivals, the Queen's entrance at St. Mary's Islington was rather quiet. While a dozen or so paparazzi flashed cameras and captured video footage, the event promised no other celebrities to capture popular attention on social media or in the evening paper. The Queen was not speaking, presenting honors, or serving as the center of attention. If she had her way, Her Majesty might likely have slipped in just as the service was starting, unannounced and unnoticed, just as she and members of the Royal Family have been known to do when attending concerts, operas, and other public performances.

She had no obligation to attend, and likely no one would

have noticed if she had chosen not to be there. The event, however, was one the Queen would not have missed. At the small neighborhood church where no monarch had set foot for over a thousand years, this service celebrated the 150th anniversary of Scripture Union, an international, interdenominational, evangelical charity founded to help children and young people grow in their faith and relationship with God. The organization's first official meeting had been held in the same neighborhood a century and a half ago, and now St. Mary's welcomed the opportunity to commemorate the contribution Scripture Union had made in Great Britain and—through international chapters in over 120 countries—around the world.

Unable to attend less conspicuously, Queen Elizabeth sat at the front of the church with other distinguished guests and service participants. She bowed in prayer, sang hymns she knew by heart, and beamed at the performance by a children's choir from St. Mary's Primary School. As a new hymn, "God of Unchanging Grace" by Bishop Timothy Dudley-Smith, rang through the church to commemorate the Scripture Union Jubilee, Her Majesty subtly nodded her approval.

While she serves as patron to more than six hundred charities, Queen Elizabeth seems especially dedicated to Scripture Union. As Reverend Tim Hastie-Smith, Scripture Union's national director, explained, "We were thrilled that Her Majesty the Queen chose to join us as we celebrated 150 years of sharing the good news and love of Jesus Christ with the children and young people of this nation. For so many young people, it is the faithful and gently inspiring witness of parents, grandparents and great-grandparents that testifies most powerfully to God's enduring love. Her Majesty embodies this witness, and just as she seeks to serve all people of this nation regardless of race or religion, so SU seeks to testify to the abiding presence of a life-transforming loving God, whose love is for all, and is found freely in His world."[1]

The contrast between that humble service and the pomp and circumstance of the one that launched Queen Elizabeth's reign could not be sharper. More than sixty years earlier, Her Majesty had attended another historic church, but at this one she could not escape being the center of attention. After all, her coronation in Westminster Abbey on June 2, 1953, was the first televised installation of a British monarch, with an estimated audience of more than twenty-five million viewers.[2]

Although Elizabeth was the star participant, she resisted televising her coronation at first. Her father had not allowed cameras into the abbey in 1937 for his coronation, which she had witnessed as an eleven-year-old princess, and she had chosen not to broadcast her wedding to Prince Philip in 1947. Apparently, she feared misspeaking or making some mistake in the nearly three-hour ceremony that would not only be televised to millions around the world but would be recorded for posterity.[3] In addition, the Queen considered parts of the service deeply personal and sacred, particularly Holy Communion and the part of the service known as "the anointing."

When the decision not to televise the coronation was announced, however, public outcry prevailed. Elizabeth remained uneasy but compromised, allowing the service to be broadcast live but without close-ups of Her Majesty's face. It was also agreed that cameras would pan away during communion and the anointing.

The live broadcast united public support for this new sovereign. The young Queen offered the promise of a new beginning, a fresh start. World War II had ended only a few years prior, and hope for establishing a new normalcy blossomed amid the rations and ravages of wartime. The three previous monarchs had been male, with George V and George VI sandwiched around the abdication of Edward VIII. In contrast, Queen Elizabeth II provided the promise of stability, vibrancy, and a reminder of past beloved queens such as Victoria and Elizabeth I, who enjoyed long, popular reigns.

Filled with pomp and circumstance dating back many centuries, the service order had changed little since the coronation of William the Conqueror, the first monarch to be crowned in Westminster Abbey, back in 1066 after his victory over the Saxons at the Battle of Hastings. For the coronation of Queen

Queen Elizabeth II taking her vows during her coronation, June 2, 1953.
Universal History Archive/Getty Images

Elizabeth II, Westminster Abbey was closed for six months before the big event in order to prepare. Railway track was installed leading directly into the ancient church to transport the tons of wood and metal required to construct new stadium-style seating. With capacity stretched from two thousand to eight thousand guests, there was nowhere to go but up!

Most of us born after this event have likely never witnessed anything comparable. Queen Elizabeth's coronation combined the history, tradition, and romanticism seen in the royal weddings of Charles and Diana, William and Catherine, and Harry and Meghan with the preparation, nationalism, and grandeur of an international Olympics. In addition, it combined the glamor of a Hollywood film premier with the community spirit of a neighborhood block party. The Queen's coronation pulled out all the stops and spared no expense. The abbey, packed to the rafters with witnesses and fragrant with fresh flowers from England, Scotland, Wales, and Ireland, became the meeting place of heaven and earth.

Almost thirty thousand soldiers from countries throughout the British Empire marched, paraded, and guarded the safety of the more than three million spectators camped out on the streets of London along the five-mile procession. The Queen rode in a solid gold carriage—dating back to King George III and exceeding anything Disney ever imagined for a princess—drawn by a team of eight gray geldings. While the weather delivered overcast skies and sporadic showers, no amount of rain could dampen the jubilant spirits celebrating Coronation Day.

Less than six months earlier, the new Queen had delivered her first Christmas address, a tradition started by her grandfather, King George V. In her address she anticipated the sacred vows she would be taking during her coronation. "I want to ask you all," she said, "whatever your religion may be, to pray for me on that day—to pray that God may give me wisdom and strength to carry out the solemn promises

I shall be making, and that I may faithfully serve Him and you, all the days of my life."[4]

Her request, and the prayers of her many subjects and admirers, apparently was answered. The service consisted of five parts—recognition, oath, anointing, crowning, and homage. However, the sacred centerpiece of the ceremony was her anointing with holy oil, a mixture of sesame seed and olive oil, perfume with roses, orange flowers, jasmine, musk, civet, and ambergris.[5] Shielded by a canopy directly above Her Majesty, the archbishop of Canterbury poured oil from the ampulla, the solid gold vessel in the shape of an eagle used only for coronations, into the spatula-shaped spoon, another priceless artifact set apart for use only on this occasion.

Dipping his finger in the holy oil, the archbishop made a cross on Elizabeth's hands, then her heart, before concluding, "Be thy head anointed with holy oil, as kings, priests and prophets were anointed. . . . As Solomon was anointed king by Zadok the priest and Nathan the prophet, so be thou anointed, blessed and consecrated Queen over the peoples whom the Lord thy God has given thee to rule and govern."

His words came from the precedent set by the earliest known coronation as recorded in the Old Testament (1 Kings 1:38–50) and consummated the intimate bond between sovereign and God, the King of Kings—and in this case, Queens. The anointing conveys the holy seal of God empowering the monarch, a meeting and mingling of the sacred and sacrificial, the eternal and the temporal, the divine and the mortal. It is simply "magic," as the duke of Windsor declares in Peter Morgan's version of events in the "Smoke and Mirrors" episode of *The Crown*.

Divinely appointed or humanly anointed, monarchs seem

to have always embodied the divine for their subjects, either as a self-proclaimed deity or as a specially chosen representative for God or gods. In the Hebrew history recorded in the Old Testament, leadership almost always involved God in some dramatic way. Generally, either kings and queens were anointed and chosen by God directly and accepted as such by those around them, or they were rebellious leaders set up to suffer the consequences of shirking their faith as well as their duty to lead by example for God's people.

We see this dichotomy in the life of Saul, who was chosen by God as the first king of Israel, signaling the transition from twelve tribes to one nation. God's prophet Samuel found Saul and informed him of God's decision, and King Saul led the people of Israel effectively until he began to disobey God and make his own decisions. This led to God's Spirit departing from Saul, which in turn ignited an ongoing depression in the king.

Then there's David, the young, plucky shepherd boy whom God chose to replace Saul, once again via a visit from the prophet Samuel. In hindsight, David's life may have been messier than Saul's, with one crucial difference: David remained a man after God's own heart. For all his mistakes—pride, adultery, murder, and abuse of royal power, to name a few—David never closed his heart to his need for God, and his willingness to serve God never waned.

The sovereign, then and thereafter in most monarchies, embodied an incarnational role as God's chosen representative to lead—and to serve—God's people. This divine responsibility precedes Queen Elizabeth's other duties to this day, as reflected in the first question asked by the archbishop of Canterbury during the oath on Coronation Day: "Will you to the utmost of your power maintain the Laws of God and the true profession of the Gospel?"[6] Commitments of intent regarding her leadership of the Church of England and the government formed by the United Kingdom's constitutional monarchy followed *after* her vow to uphold God's laws and to profess the gospel of Christ.

Such emphasis, along with her affirmation, could easily have evolved into just another perfunctory part of an ancient and arcane ceremony for British monarchs in the twentieth century. But Elizabeth's firm "I will" before her faithful subjects and the eyes of the world resounded with sincerity and humility. Her response echoed the willingness apparent in the speech she had given on her twenty-first birthday:

> I declare before you all that my whole life whether it be long or short shall be devoted to your service and the service of our great imperial family to which we all belong. But I shall not have strength to carry out this resolution alone unless you join in it with me, as I now invite you to do: I know that your support will be unfailingly given. God help me to make good my vow, and God bless all of you who are willing to share in it.[7]

When she arrived into this world on April 21, 1926, Elizabeth was the firstborn of the Duke and Duchess of York and the third grandchild of the reigning monarch, King George V, who reportedly delighted in the thoughtful, well-behaved child whispering secrets to him at family holiday celebrations and informal gatherings.

That Elizabeth, or Lilibet as she was known then, would live a life of royal privilege was a given. Like her younger sister, Margaret Rose, and cousins on her father's side, she would

enjoy a life of leisure framed by public service. But then something most unexpected forever changed the trajectory of Elizabeth's life.

Rather than basking in country life, young Lilibet quickly became a princess traversing the dark woods of the abdication crisis on an epic journey toward the light of Buckingham Palace via Westminster Abbey. Perhaps more like Odysseus than Sleeping Beauty, she faced her own internal fears as much as her

The Duchess of York looking at her newborn daughter, Elizabeth Alexandra Mary Windsor, May 1926. *Speaight/Hulton Archive/Getty Images*

external circumstances on this extended quest. Did she have what it takes to wear the crown? And what kind of person would she become while wearing it?

It did not take long to find out. When her grandfather began suffering more acutely from chronic pulmonary disease, the wheels of historic change began to turn. After King George V received a fatal injection of morphine and cocaine from the royal physician and died on January 20, 1936,[8] Elizabeth's uncle, known by the family as David and to the public as the Prince of Wales, became his father's successor, King Edward VIII—at least for most of 1936.

The less-than-a-year reign and abdication of Edward

VIII remains a fascinating pivot in British history. Forced to choose between his duty as king and his love for the American divorcée Wallis Simpson, he followed his heart and gave up the crown to be with the woman he loved. Whether viewed as a tragic, romantic sacrifice or a selfish, foolhardy mistake, Edward's abdication brought the conflict between a monarch's personal desire and public duty to a head.

His abdication also symbolizes the social, cultural, and institutional changes of his day in ways unique from any of his royal predecessors. In a post-Victorian, newly-industrial, post-war kingdom, the crisis precipitated by Edward VIII gave expression to so many timely conflicts: between church and state, public appearance and private intention, individual and institution, freedom of choice and obligation of status, ambition and aristocracy.

These tensions voiced the growing pains of a modern world.

World War I introduced a new kind of warfare that was no longer limited to remote battlefields and military chess games. The power of the church declined, while social morals loosened personal behavior from the corseted conservatism of the Victorian age. And forms and styles of art and literature evolved from what experts deemed worthy to an emphasis on individual forms of expression.

Traditional realism and naturalism shifted to more innovative, subjective styles and forms of expression. While Victorians valued conformity, consistency, and symmetry, Modern artists created unique, unexpected, unpredictable forms. It's the difference between a painting by John Everett Millais and one by Henri Matisse, between a novel by Charles Dickens and one by James Joyce.

What does all this have to do with the faith of Queen Elizabeth? Everything! Because among the tensions inherent in this cultural shift, we find a knotted conflict between personal freedom and the pull of precedent, between desire to live as one pleases and duty to live in the role prescribed for you.

If the abdication crisis epitomizes the symbolic shift of society and culture from the nineteenth century to the twentieth century, it ultimately remains a struggle between head and heart, duty and desire. Coincidentally, this battle of individual wills just happened to carry national, international, and historic consequences. In his pursuit of the personal fulfillment offered by love and marriage, King Edward VIII quickly reached an impasse of epic proportions.

In January 1936, when George V died and the Prince of Wales assumed the crown, Mrs. Wallis Simpson was still married to Ernest Simpson, a London-based shipping executive. She had met the Prince of Wales in 1931 and had become his constant companion by 1935, when the two enjoyed a holiday in Europe together, among other public appearances and private testimonials. Wildly in love with the outgoing American socialite, the new King continued their affair with abandon, intending to marry Mrs. Simpson once she divorced her husband.

During this ten-month interval, the British press did not directly address this rather delicate situation out of respect for the monarchy, which in turn kept it discreetly out of the public eye. Once Mrs. Simpson filed for divorce in October, however, the blinders were removed. King Edward's affair with her had already been reported in numerous papers and periodicals overseas, and numerous British subjects living abroad often shared their clippings back home. Perhaps the tipping point occurred when Edward informed Prime Minister Stanley Baldwin that he would be marrying Mrs. Simpson as soon as her divorce became final. Appalled by the idea, Baldwin adamantly insisted that she, as a twice-divorced American with a scandalous reputation, would never be accepted as queen. Both men refused to back down.

About two weeks after this stalemate between the King and PM Baldwin, however, a clergyman inadvertently lit the fuse on this slow-burning bombshell. Alfred Blunt, the bishop of Bradford, delivered an address at a conference in his diocese anticipating the upcoming coronation, scheduled for May the following year (1937). Calling into question the new king's moral character and personal faith, Blunt said:

> On this occasion the King holds an avowedly representative position. His personal views and opinions are his own, and as an individual he has the right of us all to be the keeper of his own private conscience. But in his public capacity at his Coronation, he stands for the English people's idea of kingship. It has for long centuries been, and I hope still is, an essential part of that idea that the King needs the grace of God for his office.
>
> First, on the faith, prayer, and self-dedication of the King himself; and on that it would be improper for me to say anything except to commend him to God's grace, which he will so abundantly need, as we all need it—for the King is a man like ourselves—if he is to do his duty faithfully. We hope that he is aware of

his need. Some of us wish that he gave more positive signs of such awareness.[9]

Before taking the throne, the Prince of Wales, as Elizabeth's Uncle David was known, had been quite the playboy. Unmarried, he enjoyed the company of women and frequented social events high and low, from aristocratic balls to basement jazz clubs. He was the first Royal to be photographed while smoking a cigarette. He chatted with reporters and photographers and charmed virtually everyone he met.

Bishop Blunt, totally unaware—along with the vast majority of British subjects—of the King's involvement with the married Mrs. Simpson, intended only to call the sovereign to a higher standard. If nothing else, the King could at least go through the motions of having a Christian faith that included regular church attendance. For the Head of the Church and Defender of the Faith, it came with the job.

But Blunt's speech ignited the powder keg of public exposure.

A reporter named Ronald Harker, from the local West Yorkshire newspaper *Telegraph & Argus*, heard Blunt and wrote up a report for the national Press Association. London reporters had played nice until then, feeling gagged by tradition, historical precedent, and British reserve. Blunt's speech was the opening they needed, enabling them to address the King's behavior without starting the conversation.

The story of the King's involvement with Mrs. Simpson broke in papers across Great Britain the following morning. Roughly half the population supported their King's rebellion against the rules of Parliament and the Church, agreeing that he had the right to marry the woman he loved regardless.

The other half, including most aristocrats and power brokers, expressed contempt at their sovereign's unwillingness to play by the rules.

Victorian duty had collided head-on with Modern desire. There was no turning back.

When Edward maintained his commitment to marry his beloved Mrs. Simpson, Prime Minister Baldwin warned the King that such action would result in the resignation of all Parliament members, guaranteeing unprecedented governmental chaos. As if to up the ante in this high-stakes game of poker, Edward threatened to abdicate. He dug in and may have expected to get what he wanted. Or, as some royal historians have speculated, his love for Wallis Simpson provided a legitimate reason to excuse himself from a job with responsibilities and obligations he found too confining.

Whatever the tangled skein of emotions might have been, Edward's insistence on pulling the thread of personal passion threatened to unravel the royal security blanket of the monarchy.

But political consultations with leaders in dominions of the British Empire—including the Irish Free State, Canada, Australia, New Zealand, and South Africa—clipped this loose thread before it went any further. Leaders of Parliament as well as their counterparts in the Commonwealth would accept no scenario involving Edward's marriage to Mrs. Simpson. As long as Wallis was his betrothed, Edward would have to choose between wearing the crown and wearing a wedding ring.

By choosing to abdicate, Edward began the process of

redefining the British monarchy, a project his niece continues to this day. As her father acceded to the throne as King George VI, Elizabeth saw firsthand and up close the steep personal price required to wear the crown. Her uncle's decision had fractured the monarchy, and now she watched her father try to repair the damage amid the turmoil of the Second World War. King George VI's reign lasted only sixteen years, his life cut short by lung cancer, as well as the stress of his responsibilities during wartime.

These variables, historical as well as personal, factored into how Elizabeth approached the call to serve. Now, after surpassing Queen Victoria as the longest-reigning British monarch, Queen Elizabeth has redefined the institution and its relevancy for our twenty-first century, tech-driven global culture. In fact, she has lived most of her life in the ever-expanding public eye, filmed on television and now featured in social media. Arguably the most famous woman in the world, she is undoubtedly the most photographed, an iconic figure for more than seven decades.

Queen Elizabeth is the only British monarch that the vast majority of people in the world, let alone the United Kingdom, have known in their lifetime. Today more articles, documentaries, and programs (including *The Crown* on Netflix and the Academy Award–winning film *The Queen*) scrutinize her and the Royal Family than ever before. But what fuels this surge of popularity and public interest?

Numerous factors contribute, including Her Majesty's intelligence, humility, humor, poise, and grace under pressure.

She is authentically herself. The Queen exudes the kind of confidence that cannot be contrived. In addition, she has sustained that poise for over seven decades and through numerous crises, both personal and political. At the heart of this confidence, we glimpse Her Majesty's personal faith in God.

More than the product of polite deference to historical tradition, the Queen's faith transcends her inherited responsibility and the theology of the Anglican Church. The faith of Queen Elizabeth shines with the luster of a lifetime serving others, refined by the fires of deep-seated struggles and polished by her humor and humility. Such an authentic faith could not be merely academic, political, or social but is undoubtedly personal, visceral, and deeply intimate.

Perhaps the Queen's faith began, as it did for many of us, as an obligation, a product of family custom and cultural tradition. Parents have been passing down their views on God, religion, and the meaning of life to their children since Adam and Eve exited Eden. Part of being human means wrestling with the existence of God, the nature of suffering, and the overall spiritual dimension to life, even if one decides not to believe any of it.

For centuries, generations around the world have been seeking a way to know God or a higher power and purpose for their lives. People used to rely on the priest, bishop, pope, and religious hierarchy to take care of their business with God. Perhaps some still do.

Historically, subjects of the Crown could also rely on the fact that the monarch, as head of state and Head of the Church, maintained the only direct relationship with God they might require. Like children resting in the comfort of their parents' provisions of food and shelter, they did not have to worry about such lofty matters as personal salvation and discovering a meaningful, transcendent purpose in life.

Martin Luther, among other Reformers, changed all that. The church no longer needed a hierarchy of gatekeepers. Clearly, personal desire could change the course of one's public duty. Although religious hierarchies certainly continued to exist then as they do now, an emphasis on one's personal relationship to God continued to grow. Individuals no longer had to trust their understanding of God, as well as their communication with him, to a special delegate, prophet, priest, or monarch.

Nevertheless, we are social creatures living in various intersecting networks of relationships. Even today most people still shape their personal faith and spirituality with input from others, especially authoritative figures who lead churches, both locally and nationally, as well as clergy, pastors, theologians, mystics, mentors, and gurus, not to mention those from history. While we have evolved in our reliance on the spiritual leadership of others to a more democratic, consumer-based approach, we still consider the ways we see other prominent people living their faith and allow them to influence our own spiritual life.

Granted, not all spiritual heroes or role models are equal, and some have even turned their influence toward accumulating personal wealth, adoration, and attention. At their worst, they become dangerous cult leaders and con artists. At their best, they restore our hope and inspire us to become better people, drawing us back again and again to God's grace, Christ's love, and the Spirit's presence in and among us.

Discerning the difference can be challenging at times. A person's faith is the most intimate aspect of a person's being, and to talk about someone else's faith seems incredibly presumptuous, potentially disrespectful, and particularly dangerous. One can never know what is in the heart of someone else, which is why such matters are indeed better left to God. Aristotle said one's character must be defined by one's actions, not one's motives or intentions. Nonetheless, we are influenced by one another's acts of faith, both within our families and communities but also historically and personally.

We admire, revere, and emulate the faith of martyrs, heroes, and underdogs of the faith such as William Wilberforce, Dorothy Day, Martin Luther King Jr., Nelson Mandela, and Mother Teresa. But what if some heroes of the faith are called to a different kind of sacrifice, a faithful dedication to service no less challenging than working with the poor of Calcutta or trying to overturn generations of social attitudes about race?

Queen Elizabeth II did not choose her role, nor did she refuse it. And she has never used her royal position as a pedestal for self-aggrandizement, self-indulgence, or self-congratulations. Instead, she has accepted her position as queen, Head of the Church of England, and Defender of the Faith solemnly and soberly. But it clearly is not duty alone driving Her Majesty's seven decades of service. Something in the fiber of her faith is clearly informed by her personal relationship with God.

Surprising as it may be to some, even as it is assumed by others, Queen Elizabeth II has much to teach us about living out our faith and following the example set by Jesus Christ. Early on she accepted the call placed on her life, yet she made that role uniquely her own by the way she has lived, served, and reigned. She discovered how to navigate safe passage between the Scylla of duty and the Charybdis of desire.

The only way to wear the royal grandeur of the monarchy was to remain clothed in her humanity. And her Christian faith remains the thread stitching person and personage, duty and desire, together.

When I began researching the Christian faith of Queen Elizabeth II, I appreciated the complexity, or near impossibility, of such a daunting quest. Nonetheless, I determined to examine the events, words, and deeds of the "world's most famous woman," as she's often called, and glean what they reveal of her faith, and what that faith has to say to us today. Also, as a fan of Peter Morgan's award-winning film *The Queen* as well as his popular, critically acclaimed Netflix series *The Crown*, I wanted to know more about Her Majesty's life and faith in order to separate fact from fiction.

A key part of my research involved spending a few weeks in the United Kingdom, not only visiting libraries, palaces, and historical sites but also talking with a handful of experts as well as many more citizens in casual settings: pubs and cafés, coffee fellowship after a church service, tourist sites, a village Christmas festival, and train rides. My findings there confirmed and enhanced my other research, and you will find these personal stories at the end of each chapter.

Without a doubt, Her Majesty Queen Elizabeth II is more popular than ever, both as an ambassador of cultural history and an emblem of national pride but also as a role model, philanthropist, iconic leader, and Christian. As one gentleman in a West End pub told me over pints at the bar one afternoon, "Her Majesty the Queen has nothing left to prove! She's the real deal, and now everyone knows it. There will never be another like her." A retired civil servant from the northern London suburb of Finchley, this man was enjoying a Guinness while waiting on his wife to finish her shopping.

He was intrigued that I would choose to focus exclusively on Queen Elizabeth's personal faith, considering it simply "part of who she is." He also confessed that he and his wife no longer attended church, except occasionally at Christmas or Easter, but that he had fond boyhood memories of visiting his grandparents in Yorkshire and attending church with them there. "My mother's parents were younger than Her Majesty, but they were from that same generation. You worked hard—not to make a lot of quid but because it was the right thing to do. It was one's duty. Today . . . well, there's a bit of slack with me kids and grandkids . . ." He shrugged, sipped his pint, and asked whether I had children.

After confirming that I do and sharing the ages and whereabouts of all three, I gently directed our conversation back to Queen Elizabeth. "I admire her faith," my new friend said, "I do. Her Christmas broadcasts always move me—silly, isn't it?—but I believe she means what she says. And then into each new year, at least for a bit, I try to be just a little kinder, more patient, a good bloke."

As our impromptu conversation ended and I thanked him for our chat, I considered his final point. It resonated with me and my desire to explore the faith of Queen Elizabeth and to shine a spotlight on what we can all learn from her example. Because at the heart of looking at someone else's faith, you often discover what it is that you yourself believe and how you also want to live out those beliefs.

I cannot lead you into battle. I do not give you laws or administer justice, but I can do something else. I can give you my heart and my devotion to these old islands and to all the peoples of our brotherhood of nations.

—annual Christmas broadcast,
1957

chapter two

COMMITMENT *and* CONVICTION

ALIGNING BEHAVIOR WITH BELIEFS

*I*n the episode *"Scientia Potentia Est"* of *The Crown*, a young Elizabeth sits thoughtfully at a desk in a cavernous classroom as a black raven dances among piles of books stacked on his master's desk at the front. She is the only pupil, and her teacher, Henry Marten, is the vice-provost of Eton College and expert on constitutional history.

"There are two elements of the Constitution," he states, "the *efficient* and the *dignified*. Which is the monarch?"

His student hesitates, distracted by the black bird.

"Your Royal Highness?" he asks, gently commanding the princess's attention.

"The dignified," she answers.

"Very good," Professor Marten confirms. "The efficient has the power to make and execute policy and is answerable to the electorate. 'What touches all should be approved by all.' The two institutions—Crown and government, the dignified and the efficient—only work when they support each other. When they trust each other. You can underline that."

And the future Queen does just that, a detail returning to sharp focus later in the episode when Her Majesty faces the dilemma of how to handle a small conspiracy of deception led by Prime Minister Churchill regarding his poor health as well as the ailing condition of Britain's foreign secretary, Anthony Eden. Feeling powerless to intervene or expose their cover-up, the young Queen Elizabeth, encouraged by the professor she has brought in to tutor her in general education, scolds the elder statesman as well as the Marquess of Salisbury in a manner that is both respectful as well as justifiably angry.

The scene is fictional, a product of writer-producer Peter Morgan's historically inspired imagination, but the dilemma is factual. Winston Churchill did indeed suffer two mild strokes that he kept hidden from Her Majesty while downplaying the gallbladder and bile duct surgery Foreign Secretary Eden required while visiting the United States. Surely, though, the Queen had to address the deception in some way, exercising her influence without interfering in the prime minister's leadership.

Considering that the British sovereign is charged with forming and influencing a government by and for her subjects, this responsibility must be one of the most challenging as well. Prime ministers are invited to serve at the pleasure of the monarch and yet rise to the position largely based on public voting and consensus within their own party. At the time of this writing, Theresa May is presently the thirteenth prime minister to serve by invitation of Her Majesty.

Of the thirteen PMs serving during Queen Elizabeth's reign, perhaps none was more influential than Sir Winston Churchill. Arguably on the downhill slope of an iconic and historic career of civil service by the time he served her, Churchill had known his new Queen since she was two years old, noting even then "an air of authority and reflectiveness astonishing for an infant."[1] During the twenty-four years that passed between that meeting and the first time Churchill attended his first weekly appointment with her, the elder statesman served under Elizabeth's father, King George VI, from 1940 until 1945 during World War II and the Blitz.

Prime Minister Winston Churchill and Lady Churchill welcome Queen Elizabeth for dinner at 10 Downing Street, 1955.
AP/Shutterstock

By the time Elizabeth acceded to the throne, Churchill had returned to 10 Downing Street in 1951. He then valued the monarchy more than ever, believing "the monarchy represented not only the apex of our society and constitutional arrangements, but a focus for the loyalty and aspirations of many millions."[2] Living a life largely devoted to service for his country, including his courageous leadership during World War II, Churchill indeed offers an expert opinion.

The great statesman had been born in 1874 and grew up during the golden years of Queen Victoria's reign, concurrent with the Gilded Age in US history. Churchill came from an affluent, aristocratic family that likely instilled in him an abiding respect for the British monarchy and an appreciation of its historical role in British government. After a distinguished military career and the beginning of a lifelong authorship, Churchill became a Member of Parliament (MP) in 1900, on the cusp of transition from Queen Victoria to her son, King Edward VII.

Churchill considered himself an agnostic, more of a "flying buttress" than a "pillar of the church," according to historian David Dilks.[3] As such, the British Bulldog, as the tenacious leader was often called, rarely called on the name of God, either casually or profanely, which serves only to magnify the extent of his heartfelt praise for his Queen near the end of his tenure as Prime Minister:

> Our Island no longer holds the same authority or power that it did in the days of Queen Victoria. A vast world towers up around it and after all our victories we could not claim the rank we hold were it not for the respect for our character and good sense and the general admiration not untinged by envy for our institutions and way of life. All this has already grown stronger and more solidly founded during the opening years of the present Reign, and I regard it as the most direct mark of God's favour we have ever received in my long life that the whole structure of our new-formed Commonwealth has been linked and illuminated by a sparkling presence at its summit.[4]

We must keep in mind this observation was made by the man who had experienced both World Wars. While many might think Britain's survival and ultimate triumph were their nation's greatest signs of God's favor, Sir Winston believed that even greater still was the gift of their young Queen.

Churchill's praise recognizes the remarkable challenge facing Queen Elizabeth II: reigning without actually ruling, influencing without directing, leading without controlling. As someone intimately acquainted with British government, Churchill knew well its idiosyncratic complexities. Simply put, Her Majesty had her work cut out for her.

Perhaps no one provides a better explanation, and exploration, of the United Kingdom's constitutional monarchy than Walter Bagehot, the nineteenth-century author of a seminal text on British government eponymously titled *The English Constitution* (1867). Relied on by historians, barristers, and politicians, Bagehot's great work became a royal primer for Elizabeth at a young age, just as it had for her father and grandfather. His contrast of the efficient and dignified elements of the British Constitution illuminates a democratic system that often confuses many outside the Commonwealth.

Sir William Anson's classic, three-volume work, *The Law and Custom of the Constitution* (1886), identifies the problem, describing the British Constitution as "a somewhat rambling structure . . . like a house which many successive owners have altered."[5] Unlike the US Constitution, which serves as the primary source for our democratic republic, the United

Kingdom has no singular, codified constitution. Instead, a collection of laws, documents, and historical provisions and precedents provide the legal, ethical, and philosophical foundation for its unique governing system.

Most schoolchildren in the US receive an explanation of our independent democratic republic as a contrast to the historical monarchies of many European countries, including Britain, with whom we fought for our independence. As they become adults and learn more, however, the distinction between our American system with a president and members of Congress and the British system with a prime minister and members of Parliament can begin to blur.

The monarchy, however, remains the crucial difference, defying contemporary logic while replacing it with a sense of something ancient and mysterious. Bagehot wrote, "The mystic reverence, the religious allegiance, which are essential to a true monarchy are imaginative sentiments that no legislature can manufacture in any people. You might as well adopt a father as make a monarchy."[6] It's as if the United Kingdom walks a high wire of governance, balancing, by design, historical monarchy on one end with contemporary democracy on the other.

If such a balancing act appears dangerously impossible to onlookers, then we can only imagine what it must be like for the sovereign embodying this concept. The great challenge for any modern British monarch, which Elizabeth II soon realized, centers on the power of Parliament, which expresses the voice and exercises the instrument of the people it serves. The phrase the future queen underlines from Bagehot in the *"Scientia Potentia Est"* episode of *The Crown*—"What touches all should be approved by all"—makes clear that this is a democratic system intended to allow majority rule. This inherently includes the likelihood that leaders, partisan powers, trends, and cultural moods will inevitably shift.

But the monarchy, the dignified facet of the government, remains constant—not only for the duration of any sovereign's reign but presumably for all time. Thus, Elizabeth, like her father and all members of her royal ancestral line, becomes a steward and ambassador of the institution, one established by God and accepted by his people. In this sense, the monarchy is not about political authority or individual personality. Nor is it about her preferences, personal expression, or for that matter, her leadership skills. Being the monarch is about serving, based on the precedents of history and tradition and the apparent will of God expressed by circumstantial evidence.

If service and stewardship define the sovereign in the British constitutional monarchy, then we might naturally wonder what actual power she possesses in this role.

Bagehot wrote, "The sovereign has, under a constitutional monarchy such as ours, three rights—the right to be consulted, the right to encourage, the right to warn."[7] Nearly a century later, British historian Robert Blake concurred: "The function of the Queen today can be divided into that of influence and that of power. . . . it also includes an almost magical symbolism of the permanence and unity of the nation."[8]

In essence, the monarch's greatest power resides in being a living symbol.

Synecdoche is a literary term rarely spoken outside of English classes and college campuses, but it's widely used by most speakers of the language. It refers to using a part to refer to the whole, such as "give me a hand." Making such a request, we would literally want more than just someone's hand; we would want their entire body, or available resources, to help us.

Derived from the Greek, with the prefix *syn* meaning "together" and *ekdoche* meaning "expectation" or "interpretation," *synecdoche* seems tailor-made for British usage in reference to its unique monarchy. In the United Kingdom, the Crown (not "a crown") has become a widely used mainstream reference for its historical monarchy as well as the reigning sovereign. To invoke another literary device, the Crown *is* the monarchy, generally as well as specifically, corporately as well as individually, conceptually and personally, both past and present. She brings multiple interpretations on an institution together in the form of one person.

Using a figure of speech such as the Crown draws on the past for its present meaning even as it is inevitably evolving with each successive sovereign. When Elizabeth was born, there was little to no serious consideration that she would one day be queen, let alone the longest-reigning monarch in British history. By laws of succession, at the time of her birth, she was third in line for the throne. Her Uncle David was the heir apparent who would succeed her grandfather, King George V, followed by her father, the Duke of York.

In 1926, the year of Elizabeth's birth, no one knew how long George V, then sixty, would live or whether David, then Prince of Wales, would marry and produce male heirs, consequently pushing Elizabeth further down the line. For that matter, her own parents might produce a male heir, which would also reduce the likelihood of her ever becoming the sovereign.

That her grandfather lived only ten more years, followed by the extraordinarily brief reign of her uncle and his unprecedented abdication, changed the chessboard of British history. In a speech to Parliament relaying King Edward VIII's decision to step down, Stanley Baldwin stressed the urgency of protecting the monarchy, saying, "The importance of its integrity is, beyond all question, far greater than it has ever been." His emphasis was not merely rhetorical in nature. In an attempt to exploit the abdication crisis, James Maxton, a socialist MP, called for a motion in Parliament to remove the monarchy and replace it with "government of a republican kind," which was defeated by a vote of 403 to 5.[9]

With the stroke of a pen when King Edward VIII gave up the throne, Elizabeth's father became King George VI, placing her as next in line. She was heir presumptive, not heir apparent, because—in theory at least—her father, forty-one, and mother, thirty-six, could produce a son, although they had no plans to extend their family beyond Elizabeth and her sister, Margaret Rose.

With her father as king on the heels of a constitutional crisis resulting in her uncle's abdication, young Elizabeth must have felt enormous pressure. On the day the brothers' transfer of power occurred, ten-year-old Lilibet informed her younger sister that their papa was now the King, to which six-year-old Margaret Rose purportedly replied, "Well poor you!"[10]

From that moment forward, Elizabeth lived with the imminent weight of her future. She knew she would someday be a living symbol, required to shepherd the historical institution of the monarchy while ensuring its survival into an uncertain future. All the more reason for her education and preparation to focus on the many facets of the crown she would one day wear in a role she had never chosen. It was, after all, her duty.

The relationship between one's beliefs and one's duty to carry them out remains at the heart of being a follower of Jesus. As the Bible makes clear:

> Do not merely listen to the word, and so deceive yourselves. Do what it says. Anyone who listens to the word but does not do what it says is like someone who looks at his face in a mirror and, after looking at himself, goes away and immediately forgets what he looks like. But whoever looks intently into the perfect law that gives freedom, and continues in it—not forgetting what they have heard, but doing it—they will be blessed in what they do. (James 1:22–25)

Beyond most Christians' attempts to act on what they believe, however, what role does this alignment play in the life of someone living in our twenty-first-century world? Is duty an outdated ideal, a social burden created by majority traditions as a tool for suppression or class limitation?

We might say one has a duty as a citizen of the United States to vote and actively participate in our democratic form of government. Similarly, traditionalists in the Christian church might teach that followers of Jesus are bound by duty to follow his example and to obey biblical principles. Most families maintain bonds of duty from parent to child and often later in reverse from adult child to aging parent.

Words such as *duty* and *obligation* carry a sense of confinement that might chafe our postmodern values of individuality and personal freedom. Responsibility entails burdens that can make us feel weighed down and trapped. We want our freedoms, especially the pursuit of happiness. Weren't the Pilgrims fleeing the class systems of the aristocracy back in England, along with the constraints of her Church, when they landed at Plymouth Rock?

Yet, ironically, the Pilgrims traded one culture's system of social restraints for their own. Although they claimed to care about religious freedom, Puritanism became what religion can become at its worst: a system based not on conformity to Christ's example but on conformity to legalism and groupthink—in other words, to religious posturing much as the Pharisees in Jesus' day. This is a harsh generalization, of course, because Puritanism influenced our country's settlers in positive ways as well, providing social order, public service, and private charity to a fledgling nation of farmers, merchants, and American dreamers.

Puritanism also set up the fundamental tension of anyone who calls themselves a Christian, which is the inherent tension of free will: the taste of forbidden fruit versus obedience to God's commands out of love, loyalty, and longing. In other words, do you do what you want to do, or do what others tell you must be done? Doing one's duty might arguably be the central conflict of humankind. The friction between personal freedom and spiritual duty often ignites sparks that illuminate the motives of our hearts.

The pressure on Queen Elizabeth II would likely be less if the monarch served only as a ceremonial or political figurehead. But as it has evolved, the British monarch must also serve as primary leader of the Church of England, thanks largely to Henry VIII and Martin Luther. Renowned theologian and minister Ian Bradley explains, "The notion of a state church with the country's ruler as its supreme governor essentially derives from the Reformation, even if it was anticipated to some extent in ancient Israel and in the Middle Ages."[11]

Prior to King Henry VIII's reign, the English Church was essentially aligned with the Catholic Church of Rome, tracing its presence on the British Isles, particularly England and Wales, all the way back to the first century, when Britain was part of the Roman Empire. By the sixth century, Pope Gregory I solidified the Vatican's relationship with Britain by choosing a Benedictine monk named Augustine to lead a mission to Britain in hopes of converting King Aethelberht, sovereign over the kingdom of Kent, from Celtic paganism to Christianity.

The King's wife, Bertha, was already a Christian, so with Augustine's influence, Aethelberht indeed followed suit, permitting the Roman missionaries to evangelize and granting them land to build a monastery just beyond the city walls of Canterbury. Augustine soon became the first bishop of Canterbury and led many of the King's subjects to join the Christian faith, most notably during Christmas Mass in 597. The Catholic Church's growth continued, and Augustine, quickly canonized after his death around 604, came to be known as the "Apostle to the English" and a primary founder of the English Church.

Nearly a thousand years later, Britain's size, both in

population and landmass, as well as the presence of the Catholic Church, had grown. Naturally, overlap existed between the authority of the king and the authority of the Church, which eventually led to a dramatic separation. But not before an important ecclesiastical designation was bestowed on the British monarch by the Church's sovereign ruler, the pope.

Among the many titles of the British sovereign, *Fidei Defensor*, Defender of the Faith, was given by Pope Leo X to Henry VIII in 1521 in honor of the king's defense of the seven sacraments of the Catholic Church as expressed in a pamphlet authored and published by His Majesty. The immense irony, of course, is that fourteen years later Henry would sever Britain's ties to Rome because Pope Clement VII, cousin of then deceased Leo, would not grant an annulment of his marriage to Catherine of Aragon. Heaping further irony on the title is the fact that Henry's chancellor, Thomas More, had ghostwritten the sovereign's famous Catholic pamphlet—the same Thomas More, celebrated centuries later in Robert Bolt's *A Man for All Seasons*, who would eventually be found guilty of treason and sentenced to death.

Another, more literal, definition of duty might illuminate the royal responsibility being exercised by Her Majesty Queen Elizabeth II throughout her reign. Duty sometimes refers to a tax, the kind often placed on imported goods or expensive items declared at customs from an exotic vacation. A duty tax is paid in order to complete ownership of an item, perhaps something luxurious or nonessential, within a certain country, state, or region.

Similarly, Queen Elizabeth has been taxed by the enormous duty that comes from wearing the crown. The incredible privilege of her sovereignty is undeniable, but its service is not without considerable cost. When she took her vows at her coronation service, she likely did not realize the full cost of personal freedoms, privacy, and normalcy she was, in effect, sacrificing, just as no one choosing to practice their faith as a believer and follower of Jesus Christ can know the full cost of their commitment or the trials they will inevitably endure.

Considering her personality and natural disposition, Queen Elizabeth II does not appear to be someone who complains or indulges in any form of self-pity. If she were so inclined, it would likely only provoke sharp rebuke and cries of outrage because of the immense wealth and privilege her status also carries. Nonetheless, she has surely been forced to sacrifice any semblance of a "normal life," one based on relative anonymity and the personal freedoms most of her subjects take for granted.

Arguably, Her Majesty has never lived a so-called normal life, but that doesn't mean she hasn't longed for a quieter, freer, more private lifestyle. Several years ago author William Kuhn wrote a charming novel called *Mrs. Queen Takes the Train* in which he imagines the accidental adventure Her Majesty enjoys when she strolls outside palace gates in search of a little fun. Feeling restless as she considers the confines of her regimented life, the Queen sneaks away to Scotland to visit a special place with many happy memories—the royal yacht, *Britannia*, retired from service and moored near Edinburgh. As she enjoys her excursion in relative anonymity, her courtiers and staff discover her absence and scramble to find her.

Much of the novel's poignancy and humor emerge from the contrast between the Queen's life as sovereign and the life she has sacrificed to wear the crown. From enjoying a train ride to having a good chat over a cup of tea with friendly strangers, she recognizes the simple pleasures and everyday moments that she gave up to serve as monarch. There's no sense of unrealistic regret or wistful nostalgia for the life she never lived, only the joy and appreciation of reveling in it while on holiday from her role—no, from her primary identity—as Britain's queen.

Similar to the kind of liberties taken by *The Crown* in connecting the dots of historical fact with true-to-character fiction, this novel provides insight that seems quite feasible, likely, even probable. By all accounts, Queen Elizabeth is a no-nonsense, practical, diligent person who thrives on routine and takes her responsibilities very seriously.

Nonetheless, she has also revealed herself to be quite human—in her compassion for others, her dedication to worthwhile causes, her love of dogs and horses, and in her quick wit and appreciation of humor. She has *worked* at being the monarch, embracing the job and making it the essence of who she is as a leader—and a public servant. One suspects her brand of hard work and dedication would result in success in any field she had chosen, whether as a diplomat, philanthropist, or corporate executive, because she fulfills the job descriptions for these three professions and many more—including historian, brand manager, lobbyist, actress, and advocate.

The ability to keep a commitment seems to depend on the depth of the conviction on which it's based. For Queen Elizabeth II, her beliefs are deeply rooted not only in the history and tradition of the British monarchy but more importantly in the Word of God. She considers her service as much obedience as offering. Does such a belief make it any easier to serve as Britain's longest-reigning monarch?

One young woman I met in London during my research visit seems to think so. We chatted in the small café operating out of St. John the Baptist Church, Parish of Holland Road, Kensington, where she worked. I happened to be there because I was staying in accommodations nearby and couldn't help but notice the beautiful, historic church nestled among quaint flats and renovated rentals. A small sandwich board advertised breakfast in the café operated by the church, and wanting an excuse to see the inside of the grand neo-Gothic structure, I went in, hoping the rain would end before I resumed my walk to Shepherd's Bush tube stop.

The dark interior revealed a beautiful small cathedral, which I learned had been designed by the famous Victorian architect James Brooks and built in 1868. Later I would discover on the church website that the church was constructed on land donated by the Holland Estate, "with the requirement that it must be made of good stone, not brick," which was apparently the popular building material at the time. I also learned St. John's held a once closely guarded secret: the Chapel of the Blessed Sacrament. The Chapel kept a reserve of the Blessed Sacrament, consecrated bread used for holy communion, which was not allowed within the Church of England.

St. John's is also well known for the role it played in the

Anglo-Catholic movement. There remain deep Catholic roots within the Church of England that found revival in the Anglo-Catholic movement, which gained significance during the nineteenth century. To recognize its role, as well as its beauty and historical significance, St. John's was granted Grade I status by the English Heritage, designating it a church "of exceptional interest and outstanding importance."[12]

While much of the church sanctuary held scaffolding for an ongoing renovation, a cavernous area near the front entry, originally part of the vestibule, had been converted into the café. The young woman, I'll call her Gemma, served as hostess, cook, server, and cashier, and that morning I was the only customer. I ordered scrambled eggs on toast along with a cup of tea with a splash of milk and took in the dank, castlelike—though not unpleasant—ambiance. Soon Gemma served me a plate of food that proved more delicious than imagined: eggs scrambled perfectly on grilled brown bread with a small side salad of arugula and split cherry tomatoes drizzled with balsamic dressing. Simple, familiar, and exotic all at once!

As I enjoyed my breakfast, Gemma tidied up the kitchen before returning to sit at the table next to mine, where she resumed reading a paperback Jeffrey Archer novel. She seemed to enjoy the quiet and simplicity of her job, which apparently didn't see many patrons. She possessed a natural poise and intelligent demeanor and dressed simply in jeans and a blue sweater (or jumper, as the Brits say). She could easily have passed for a university student.

I complimented her on my eggs, toast, and salad and hoped she might be willing to chat with me about her sovereign's faith. While I suspect at first she was just being polite to the rather academic-looking American old enough to be her father, she soon warmed to our discussion. She had just graduated from a respectable city college six months earlier and would be starting a graduate program in business at a more prestigious university in January, then only a few weeks away. Her focus was on fashion marketing and branding, and I was quite impressed by how confident and self-assured she seemed. When I told her as much, she smiled shyly before admitting, "Thanks—suppose that's how I should sound at this point. But, honestly, I'm not sure what I want to do . . ."

I shared how natural it was to be uncertain and described the tentative paths my three young adult children had recently embarked on. "What are you most passionate about?" I asked. "What is it about marketing that intrigues you?"

Her dark eyes searched mine before she leaned forward and said, "Design! I'm actually much more interested in fashion *design*—creating beautiful clothes from start to finish—than marketing. But design's such an *impossible* field. There's no way to break into such a crowded market. Much easier just to focus on promoting other designers."

She then asked about my profession and what had brought me to London, which permitted a segue to my writing this book. "What do you think of Queen Elizabeth's fashion?" I began.

Gemma smiled and said, "Actually, she does quite well! It's not my taste—much too posh and conservative—but it works for her. She knows who she is and looks comfortable in the role. I believe that's an enormous part of what fashion is about."

"Have you ever thought much about Her Majesty's faith?"

She thought for a moment and sighed, "Honestly, no,

I haven't really. It's just not . . . well, I don't think much about God, I suppose."

"So do you attend St. John's?" I asked. "Or does your family?"

"Neither," she said, smiling sheepishly. "My mother has a friend in the congregation here. I just needed a part-time job before grad school next year, so . . ."

"Of course," I nodded and then stood, cueing Gemma to return behind the counter so she could ring me up. I paid and told her to keep the change.

"Good luck with your book," she said. "I do admire the way the Queen has always been true to herself. I don't know if that has much to do with faith or not. But it's clear she believes in what she's doing—and why she's doing it."

"Indeed, she does," I agreed. "Good luck to you as well. And, forgive me, but I think you should be a fashion designer, not a marketer. Don't pursue something that merely frames what you care most about. Don't be afraid to commit to your dream!"

Gemma tilted her head and smiled, the hint of a blush rising. "Thank you," she said softly. As I turned to walk out the door, her voice grew louder, "Maybe I will. Cheers!"

*At the heart of our faith stand
not a preoccupation with our own
welfare and comfort but the concepts
of service and of sacrifice.*

—*General Synod Inauguration address,
2010*

chapter three

SERVICE *and* SACRIFICE

SHOWING HUMILITY AND RESPECT
TOWARD ALL PEOPLE

*D*uring the year of her Diamond Jubilee, 2012, which celebrated her sixty years on the throne, Queen Elizabeth participated in numerous events, parties, dedications, and receptions, both public and private, to mark the momentous occasion. In the midst of this Jubilee year celebration, a label that she herself noted was drawn from the Old Testament practice (Leviticus 25:1–4; 8–10), she gave her first major public address at Lambeth Palace, official residence of the archbishop of Canterbury, located just a few hundred yards across the Thames from the Palace of Westminster, where both Houses of Parliament meet.

There Her Majesty inspired an audience of leaders from Britain's nine leading religions, including Buddhism, Judaism, Islam, and Hinduism. Her theme fit the occasion, offering a message deeply personal, explicitly faith-based, and clearly inclusive. She stressed the Church of England's responsibility and privilege to cooperate with such a rich multiethnic and multifaith society. "The Church has a duty to protect the free practice of all faiths in this country," she said before going on to emphasize "the responsibilities we have beyond ourselves." The Queen concluded, "This occasion is thus an opportunity to reflect on the importance of faith in creating and sustaining communities all over the United Kingdom. Faith plays a key role in the identity of many millions of people, providing not only a system of belief but also a sense of belonging."[1]

While over-the-top celebrations would culminate a few months later during a four-day Diamond Jubilee festival in June, Her Majesty chose to begin her milestone celebration in her role as Head of the Church of England. Her humble call to action illuminated the occasion, not her own achievements or those of the Church. Well aware of the intense public scrutiny she has received her entire life, she prioritized her point by *not* making the event about herself.

Queen Elizabeth subtly reminded British subjects, along with well-wishers around the world, of the secret to her success: her Christian beliefs and personal faith. The archbishop at that time, Dr. Rowan Williams, pointed this out by light-heartedly commenting on the way Queen Elizabeth has shown that "being religious is not eccentric or abnormal."[2] The audience laughed and nodded their assent.

Several weeks later, just as Jubilee events began to increase by the end of March, Queen Elizabeth chose another sacred event to showcase the humility and respect for others that have become hallmarks of her reign. At St. George's Chapel in Windsor,

Her Majesty held a memorial service to honor the ten-year anniversary of the deaths of both her mother and her sister.

With Elizabeth by her side, the Queen Mother had died in 2002, just shy of her 102nd birthday, passing away peacefully in her sleep, likely from a cold that had lingered for several months. Seven weeks prior, Princess Margaret had died in the hospital at the age of seventy-one, after suffering numerous strokes and additional health problems for several years. So close together, the losses compounded one another, reminding Her Majesty of the fragility of life and the importance of family. Therefore, Queen Elizabeth's holding a joint service commemorating the decade since their passing was not surprising.

What some might have found unexpected, however, was the guest list for this small, private occasion. Among the dukes and duchesses and members of the Royal Family, including Prince Philip, Prince Charles, and the Duchess of Cornwall, those in attendance by invitation of Her Majesty included "hairdressers, manicurists, maids, and horse trainers,"[3] along with William Shawcross, the Queen Mum's biographer, and playwright Tom Stoppard and actress Felicity Kendal, close friends of Princess Margaret.[4]

The mood of the service, while appropriately respectful, was uplifting and celebratory. The Dean of Windsor, the Right Reverend David Conner, officiated and began by noting, "Each of us here this morning will cherish some special personal memories, memories that awaken once again sentiments of affection and respect." He went on to praise the two departed royal women for their "faithfulness to the nation" and the ways they "significantly enriched" the lives of everyone they touched.[5]

The anniversary could easily have gone unnoticed by the public, and the service could have remained smaller and more intimate with only a few immediate family members. But Queen Elizabeth clearly wanted to remember and to celebrate the lives of these two beloved, powerful women. Her Majesty not only honored them that day, but she also invited those individuals closest to her mother and her sister, the members of staff and providers of personal service who had grown close to the Queen Mother and Princess Margaret over the years. There was no sense of rank and station; all were united by their shared losses.

After the memorial service, Queen Elizabeth hosted a reception at Windsor Castle for all guests and, according to those in attendance, seemed to especially enjoy the gathering. Her good mood was not dampened when a guest questioned the absence of William and Catherine, the Duke and Duchess of Cambridge, who were on a ski holiday in Switzerland. Unflappable, the Queen replied with a hint of a smile that she had encouraged her grandson, who had just returned from duty as a Royal Air Force helicopter pilot in the Falklands, to enjoy the reunion with his bride of less than a year. "You have something more important than this," Her Majesty had reportedly insisted.[6]

As William's Queen, she could easily have required his attendance. Instead, she focused on making the event a true celebration of life, not a solemn, requisite obligation. Consistently, Her Majesty has put people above protocol as much as possible, yet one more way she has reinvented the monarchy through her humanity and spirituality.

Elizabeth's parents surely instilled this personal brand of humble, respectful faith in her during her upbringing. While their two daughters had to be educated on etiquette befitting their royal status, they were also made to see and appreciate the universal bonds all people share. Particularly during World War II, when Elizabeth and Margaret lived at Windsor, they realized that their disruption was small compared with those families losing homes and loved ones during the London Blitz.

Windsor Castle, where the Royal Family resided during the London Blitz, January 1941.
AP/Shutterstock

Always an intelligent, dutiful child, Elizabeth grew closer to her father as she watched him face the daunting challenges presented by wearing the crown. Forced to accept the throne upon his brother's abdication, King George VI, also known as Albert or "Bertie" by family and confidantes, faced battles within and without. His brother David, then Prince of Wales, had been the heir apparent to their father, George V, and possessed the requisite presence, charm, and confidence for the role, unfazed by the stern, demanding gaze of their father.

Albert, on the other hand, wilted during his boyhood when commanded to "man up" by his father. Shy and reserved, the second in line to the throne developed a stutter at a young age, perhaps as a result of the traumatic bullying by his father, which only compounded the problem when he was then teased, often by his brother, for his inability to speak without stammering. Albert gradually learned to relax and speak with ease in private situations with those he trusted but continued to struggle with a stutter any time public pressure increased.

While he was Duke of York and second to the throne behind his older, charismatic brother, the stutter remained an occasional inconvenience. But as the new King was forced to mend the monarchy after his brother's abdication while the country teetered precipitously on the brink of another world war, Albert's stutter became a serious liability. The public, unfortunately, had already discovered Albert's nervous habit when he delivered the closing address at the British Empire Exhibition at Wembley in 1925.

In fact, it was this disastrous performance that sent Albert's wife, Elizabeth, in search of a new solution. Numerous therapies and treatments, including rolling marbles in the mouth while speaking, had already been tried unsuccessfully. At that time stuttering was considered a form of "mental weakness" or soft character, which likely didn't help matters. The Duchess of York's search yielded a meeting with Lionel Logue, an Australian would-be speech therapist and former actor, in his Harley Street office.[7]

Albert reluctantly agreed to meet with Logue, which proved the rocky start of what evolved into a professional relationship and lasting friendship, as later depicted in the Academy Award–winning film *The King's Speech*. Logue took a psychotherapeutic approach, recognizing both the physical challenges as well as the psychosomatic elements. They met regularly for nearly a year, with the unorthodox therapist supervising exercises for the future king that included singing his words instead of speaking them as well as listening to music with headphones while reading aloud, a therapeutic exercise now known as "masking."

In addition to these exercises, Logue also forced Albert to connect with him on a human level, calling him "Bertie" instead of "Your Royal Highness" or "Duke." The wily teacher insisted as well that they meet in his rather modest office in north London rather than at a royal residence or Buckingham Palace. The peculiar therapy and personal relationship instilled Albert with both the techniques and confidence to manage his handicap for the decade that followed.

His greatest test, however, came shortly after his coronation, when Britain entered the war. The new King was forced to deliver this dire news to his subjects and the world via radio, making this likely the most important speech of his reign. To hesitate or stammer would convey fear and weakness, the exact opposite of what the King wanted to communicate. A publicity photo of this event shows King George VI in his Royal Naval uniform, sitting at his desk in the palace before a large microphone.

The actual address was much more nerve-racking, with the King standing at a lectern in a small anteroom, his jacket off and the window cracked. No one was permitted in the room with him except Logue, his trusted ally by this time, who encouraged his star pupil to imagine delivering the address only to him, not to the millions listening in live across the nation and around the world. By all accounts, the speech was calm, authoritative, and appropriately solemn, a huge success that resulted in Logue congratulating not his friend Bertie, but "Your Majesty."[8]

Watching her father conquer his lifelong battle with a speech impediment surely inspired the future queen to appreciate the importance of persistence and patience. It's been suggested that the King's ability to control his speech became a metaphor for the calm, willful endurance that allowed the British people to persevere through the war. It may sound far-fetched, but there's merit to such a comparison.

The numerous ironies related to the King's nervous habit must have seemed like a cruel fate at times. Thanks to being born a second son, he never expected to wear the crown, so his stutter didn't matter—until it did. Suddenly, his brother's charm and confidence became self-absorption and petulance, and Albert's shyness and diffidence had to take their place as the foundation for a crumbling institution. The actor perfect for the part banished himself, leaving someone quite his opposite to serve as understudy, someone who not only detested the spotlight but couldn't even pronounce the *k* in *king*.

The timing of Albert's entrance must have felt quite cruel as well. For the first time in British history, the monarch could speak to all subjects at once through the new wireless technology of radio. For King George VI, this required that not only must he appear strong and royal, but he must also sound like a king on the popular new home sets. In case this pressure was not enough, his broadcasts could not be prerecorded—which would have allowed for editing and correcting flubs—because such technology was not yet available. Instead, he had to broadcast live, ensuring every syllable was heard exactly as spoken.

The final irony is perhaps the most painful of all. Among the many popular treatments for stuttering, smoking was touted as a useful diversion. As a result, the King chain-smoked most of his adult life and died of cancer at age fifty-six. Arguably, his stutter posed an ongoing challenge that could easily have left him bitter, defeated, and reclusive. Instead, King George VI rose to the occasion by refusing to yield to circumstances, even against formidable odds.

He became a symbol of the indefatigable British fighting spirit that helped defeat Germany and save the world. Dealing with something so personal, a struggle that could not be hidden once he was thrust onto the throne, Elizabeth's father taught her that one can allow circumstances to humiliate oneself and accept defeat or to humble oneself and emerge stronger. He chose the latter and brought Britain through one of the darkest chapters in her storied history.

Her father was not the only role model who showed Elizabeth the importance of service and sacrifice. In addition to her father and mother, she also found an extraordinary beacon of the Christian faith in the life of her great-great-grandmother, Queen Victoria. The longest-reigning British monarch prior to Elizabeth II, Queen Victoria provided an extraordinary model of servant leadership, one clearly founded on her devout Christian faith.

"Since it has pleased Providence to place me in this station, I shall do my utmost to fulfill my duty towards my country;

I am very young and perhaps in many, though not in all things, inexperienced, but I am sure that very few have more real good will and more real desire to do what is fit and right than I have," wrote Victoria in her journal, dated June 20, 1837, the day she became queen after her uncle, William IV, died.[9]

Serving as monarch for more than six decades, Victoria is remembered for many facets of her historic reign during the British Empire's imperial century, the period from roughly 1815 to 1915 when it colonized nearly a quarter of the world. She is also known for being a strict moralist and the catalyst for what has come to characterize the entire period named for her: propriety, obedience, self-discipline. In fact, the modern stereotype of the quintessential Brit—proper, reserved, stoic—most likely first emerged from the Victorian era.

Perhaps more a product of the times than of her personal faith, Victoria's moralistic conduct nonetheless included an attitude of service, charity, and evangelism. For many years she led a Bible study for the children of her servants and the staff at Buckingham Palace. Her church attendance exceeded her ceremonial duties as sovereign and included active ministry to the poor, the sick, and those in need.

Victoria's daughter recounted an incident in which they were strolling through nearby gardens and learned that the owner of a cottage they passed was quite ill. Concerned, the Queen returned the next day, making it clear her visit was not as royalty but as a "good Christian woman." She then pulled a Bible from a shelf in the other woman's home and read from chapter 14 of John's gospel before concluding, "Put your trust in Jesus and you will soon be in a land where there is no pain. You are a widow, so am I; we shall soon meet our beloved ones."[10]

In addition to her evangelical zeal, Queen Victoria was also known for her deep, abiding devotion to her husband and royal consort, Prince Albert, who died at the relatively young age of forty-two. During their more than twenty years of marriage, they shared a fervent Christian faith along with similar values on service and philanthropy, which they instilled in their nine children. After studying Royal Archives from the Victorian era, Yale research scientist Frank Prochaska observes, "Royal descent became not so much a title to enjoyment as a summons to duty. . . . Members of the royal family inherited charitable responsibilities the way poor children inherited clothes."[11]

Queen Elizabeth II clearly embraced the service-minded legacy of her great-great-grandparents even as she continues to pass it on to her own children, grandchildren, and great-grandchildren.

While ancestors such as her great-great-grandmother and her father, along with the Queen Mother, provided a foundational model for exercising Christian respect toward all people, perhaps Queen Elizabeth II's real proving ground for exercising this virtue has been her role as Head of the Commonwealth. Even the title itself reflects the inherent challenges of such a position.

At its peak, early in the twentieth century, the British Empire occupied around a quarter of the landmass on the planet. The sun indeed never set on the largest colonial empire in history with the Union Jack flying over portions of the five major continents—Africa, Asia, America, Australia, and Europe—along with numerous islands around the world.

When World War II broke out, the British Commonwealth—as the collective of states, territories, and countries was known—remained united by "blood, battles and bullish self-confidence," according to Dr. Harshan Kumarasingham, a contemporary lecturer in British politics at the University of Edinburgh.[12]

But even before the end of WWII, the empire began to crumble, suffering numerous cracks in its global foundation for a variety of reasons both great and small. After years of civil disobedience and nonviolent resistance to British rule, India, often considered the empire's crown jewel, was granted its independence by Parliament in 1947. Consequently, Elizabeth's father, King George VI, relinquished his title as emperor of India, but with the new nation desiring to remain a voluntary, largely symbolic, member of the Commonwealth, the challenge became finding a suitable moniker to replace it.

After "King of the Commonwealth" and "Lord Protector" were rejected as being either too imperial or too papal, the benign "Head of the Commonwealth" was finally agreed on. Much of the problem stemmed from the precedent being set when, not if, other members of the Commonwealth established their independence. The Queen's former private secretary, Michael Adeane, would later describe this solution as a "fragile flower," a metaphor reflecting both the title's decorative and tentative qualities.[13]

In the aftermath of WWII, George VI had little time to devote to this new, evolving role, a task that fell to Queen Elizabeth upon her accession in 1952. If becoming the living symbol of Britain's constitutional monarchy seemed fraught with nuanced challenges, then serving as Head of the Commonwealth was even more nebulous. On the one hand, the Queen would have to balance British nationalists keen on stressing domestic issues as her only priority, while on the other, she would need to navigate an intricate labyrinth of political, social, economic, and cultural complexities. As the English constitutional scholar Geoffrey Marshall observed, the evolving, new Commonwealth was basically a "remarkable piece of pragmatic nonsense."[14]

When Queen Elizabeth II pledged her coronation vows in 1953, she presided over more than seventy Commonwealth territories overseas. In addition to India's independence, by then British troops were trying to suppress, unsuccessfully, similar movements in Egypt and Kenya. World War II had forever changed countries and cultures, and the Cold War was dawning. Without a job description or explicit authority of any kind, Her Majesty faced a minefield of hidden motives, competing agendas, and international power plays.

During the decades that followed, the Commonwealth continued its transformation from colonized outposts of a global empire to decolonized republics in a historic alliance. Racial and cultural tensions factored heavily into what the new Commonwealth would become, with British leaders such as Leo Amery, a journalist and Tory politician, worrying whether "one of these days republicanism may become the black man's slogan" while "all whites stand together as monarchists."[15] As a result of such worries, many British subjects considered the Commonwealth a no-win endeavor, with the monarch either serving as a kind of painful reminder of imperialistic power and greed or as a farcical figurehead dispensing feel-good slogans amid an international firing squad.

Fortunately, the Commonwealth, and Elizabeth II's role

in it, has proven to be neither archaic nor embarrassing. Instead, in her typical, indomitable way, Her Majesty has shepherded an alliance of often-disparate governments, individually at various stages of national development, and created a model for cooperation, collaboration, and civility. She herself would celebrate this phenomenon "from a unique position of advantage" in her address before Parliament commemorating her Silver Jubilee celebration in 1977, noting witness to "the last great phase of the transformation of the Empire into Commonwealth and the transformation of the Crown from an emblem of dominion into a symbol of free and voluntary association. In all history, this has no precedent."[16]

It's difficult to identify just how Queen Elizabeth has managed to unite and transform the Commonwealth. Among many factors, events, personalities, and incidents, though, the main ingredient remains clear: simply put, *she cares*. Her youth became an advantage as she, like so many leaders of the newly independent Commonwealth members, matured into her role by cultivating relationships over time. Former secretary-general for the Commonwealth Sonny Ramphal observed, "Her success in Commonwealth countries has derived from an awareness that she cared—that they mattered in a sense beyond the British government. She grew up with them, understood them and related to them."[17]

In so doing, Her Majesty has managed to define a role for herself previously absent in the monarchy. She has used the lack of explicit job responsibilities to her advantage and focused on shared opportunities for growth through economic and educational development. The Queen has used her unique freedom as Head of the Commonwealth to engage with people worldwide at a level that transcends photo ops and political correctness. Long before Tony Blair called Diana the "People's Princess," Elizabeth II already served as the People's Queen.

Examples of her engagement, interaction, and advocacy for the broad spectrum of people within the Commonwealth abound. The connections Her Majesty forged often caused friction at home, most notably during the tenure of Prime Minister Margaret Thatcher. As South Africa, a member of the Commonwealth, resisted abolishing apartheid, many fellow members urged economic sanctions as a pressure point, which then Secretary-General Ramphal advocated. But Mrs. Thatcher believed such sanctions by the UK would only serve to punish South Africa's poor while impairing Britain's business interests. This opposing tension left Queen Elizabeth in the middle, torn between her roles as sovereign and Head of the Commonwealth.

With the annual Commonwealth Summit scheduled to meet in Delhi, India, in 1983, the tension over the situation with South Africa produced ripples throughout the other Commonwealth members, compounded by a variety of stakeholders. Adding to the tension was a chaotic lack of organization by the summit host country. While Queen Elizabeth highly regarded Indian Prime Minister Indira Gandhi, Her Majesty suffered numerous missteps by other Indian officials. For instance, when Hindu astrologers considered the touchdown time for the Queen's flight "inauspicious," officials refused permission for her plane to land, forcing the pilot to accommodate.

Of greater concern to Her Majesty was an administrative obstacle blocking plans for the Queen's meeting to honor Mother Teresa. Indian officials refused permission for

Queen Elizabeth to present the Order of Merit to the Nobel Prize–winning nun and future saint in the Catholic Church, citing that such a ceremony violated rules of conduct in the presidential palace, where the event was to be held. "What was supposed to be one of the highlights of the royal visit turned to farce when the Indian government intervened," reports royal expert Robert Hardman.[18] Undeterred and as resourceful as ever, Queen Elizabeth chose not to engage in a fruitless quarrel with her hosts and instead met with Mother Teresa in the garden, which in the end seemed a much lovelier, and more fitting, place for the presentation.

Prior to touching down in India for the Commonwealth Summit, Queen Elizabeth had spent four days in Bangladesh, where she encountered an impoverished, obviously malnourished child named Jamal at an orphanage outside Dhaka, the capital city. Visibly moved by the boy, Her Majesty promised that her daughter, Princess Anne, then president of Save the Children, would visit soon as part of a trip already planned. The Queen made good on her promise, with Princess Anne visiting the orphanage several times in the months and years that followed and providing assistance for the children there.

The Queen's travels as well as her meeting with Mother Teresa and tiny Jamal made such an impression on Her Majesty that they obviously inspired her message for that year's annual Christmas broadcast:

> . . . In spite of all the progress that has been made the
> greatest problem in the world today remains the gap

between rich and poor countries, and we shall not begin to close this gap until we hear less about nationalism and more about interdependence.

One of the main aims of the Commonwealth is to make an effective contribution towards redressing the economic balance between nations.

What we want to see is still more modern technology being used by poorer countries to provide employment and to produce primary products and components, which will be bought in turn by the richer countries at competitive prices.[19]

While the address was well received by most subjects, conservatives and right-leaning newspapers clamored that the Queen was too political, too egalitarian, and too biased in her usually subtle point of view. Many accused her of a thinly veiled attack on Mrs. Thatcher and claimed she was voicing the agenda of the Commonwealth's secretary-general, Ramphal. They worried Her Majesty was putting the needs and interests of other countries before those of her homeland.

The outcry echoed so long and loud that the palace did something it rarely does, issuing a statement to address the Queen's intentions. Her press secretary at the time, Michael Shea, said, "The Christmas broadcast is a personal message to her Commonwealth. The Queen has all her people at heart, irrespective of race, creed, or colour."[20]

In case the message wasn't clear, several years later Queen Elizabeth herself would provide insight to her view of the Commonwealth as well as her role in it: "If we are sometimes critical of each other, or disappointed, it is because we expect more of members of our family than we do of others. . . .

This illustrates perfectly the nature of the underlying bond which distinguishes the Commonwealth from all other international organizations."[21]

In Her Majesty's role as Head of the Commonwealth, the "fragile flower" has not only bloomed—it has flourished.

I know of no better practitioner of Queen Elizabeth's model of inclusive generosity and mutual respect than Andrew Pratt, a "retired copper looking to make a difference," as he describes himself. Andy and I have been friends for almost a decade after meeting at the Greenbelt Festival, an annual celebration of arts, faith, and justice that brings together an eclectic, ecumenical assortment of artists, activists, and authors.

Impressed with Andy's kindness and unflappable spirit, I struck up a friendship that has resulted in numerous visits on both sides of the Atlantic. Among those occasions, my wife and I were delighted to host Andy and his wife, Heather, one summer, particularly enjoying their exuberant participation in our small-town Fourth of July parade. I confess I am awed by Andy's Christian faith and inspired by his generous spirit, particularly after learning of his lengthy career in law enforcement.

Since retiring from the Lancashire Constabulary in 2010 at the rank of superintendent, a significant and prestigious post he modestly downplays, he has volunteered throughout his community there in the Northwest. He presently serves as interfaith advisor for the bishop of Blackburn. After an unsuccessful run as the Conservative party candidate for Lancashire's police and crime commissioner in 2016, Andy is considering another foray.

During my research trip to the UK, Andy and Heather kindly hosted me for a long weekend and included me in their church choir's community caroling event that Sunday afternoon in early December. Andy and I had spent considerable time comparing our respective country's political systems and leadership long before I examined Queen Elizabeth's faith. He clearly admires Her Majesty's devotion to the Church and her dedication to causes that unite rather than divide people.

"She is simply an exceptional Christian, which in turn makes her an incredible sovereign," Andy said one evening as we chatted after tea. "She is the glue that holds the Commonwealth together. With so many very different cultures, it could easily have fallen apart. When I worked on the counterterrorism initiative in London, it was so easy to see how fear was making so many people more insular and defensive, biased against immigrants and anyone they viewed as an outsider. Her Majesty the Queen, however, has never been one of those people."

As we enjoyed a small after-dinner whiskey, Andy described how he had participated in a Remembrance Day parade a few years ago in honor of his father, Warrant Officer Jim Pratt, a fighter pilot in WWII who also had the privilege of piloting a jet in the Coronation Flypast in 1953. "When I marched past Her Majesty the Queen, I'm sure she waved at me just as she had waved at Dad all those years ago," he added mischievously.

When I pressed him on why he believes Her Majesty's Christian faith matters, Andy said, "I've thought a great deal about this since you told me you were doing a book, and I believe it's really quite simple. She practices what others only preach."

I know of no single formula for success.
But over the years I have observed that some
attributes of leadership are universal and are often
about finding ways of encouraging people to combine
their efforts, their talents, their insights, their
enthusiasm and their inspiration to
work together.

—*speech to the United Nations*
General Assembly,
2010

chapter four

CONVICTION *and* COMPROMISE

GROWING THROUGH PRIVATE AND PUBLIC CRITICISM

$\mathcal{Q}$ueen Elizabeth likely had no idea that within minutes of her coronation in 1953, the seeds of her first great constitutional crisis were being sown only a few yards away. As the Royal Family's entourage departed Westminster Abbey, the Queen's younger sister, single and twenty-three, casually reached her gloved hand to the uniformed chest of a royal staff member to remove a speck. In a seemingly inconsequential gesture that could just as easily have gone unnoticed, Princess Margaret glided her finger over the row of military medals pinned above the breast pocket of Group Captain Peter Townsend, the Royal Air Force war hero newly appointed as comptroller of the Queen Mother's household.

The familiar, slightly possessive way she touched Townsend's medals did not go unnoticed, however, amid the sea of reporters covering the coronation. Any concerns they may have held about what to cover after the successful coronation immediately vanished. Here was a story sure to sell: circumstantial speculation—and eventual confirmation—that the beautiful young princess, always a maverick foil to her dutiful older sister, was in love with a divorced man sixteen years her senior.

While their relationship might not sound like a major problem for the new queen, it inevitably required Elizabeth to examine her loyalties to family in light of her duty to the Crown. Any faith worth having, it's been said, must learn to bend without breaking, and Her Majesty soon found hers pulled in opposing directions between conviction and compromise. She could be a loving, supportive big sister or a strong, unyielding Defender of the Faith. But not both.

By the time Margaret plucked the fluff from Townsend's uniform, she had known him for almost a decade. A renowned fighter pilot during World War II, he returned a highly decorated, nerve-shattered veteran, perfect qualifications for becoming King George VI's equerry, the male version of a lady-in-waiting. Originally, Townsend was to serve for three months but got along so well with the King, who so appreciated both Townsend's lingering battle trauma as well as the veteran's calm manner, that he became "equerry of honour" and served for over a decade.

In essence, Townsend became the son King George never had but longed for, a male companion who not only understood the pressure on the monarch but who also enjoyed taking care of travel details and administrative matters related to palace staff. Townsend's gentle charisma and intelligent manner gradually became indispensable, and he was promoted to deputy master of the household, an even more arduous role with numerous demands and requiring travel with the King and Royal Family for every event, holiday, or official excursion. The decorated veteran was virtually accepted as part of the family, reflected by their use of his Christian name, and obviously spent considerable time with the teenage Princess Margaret, who was only fourteen when they first met.

By both their accounts, their attraction matured into professed love during a season when they were both quite vulnerable. Princess Margaret, many years later, told royal historian Ben Pimlott, "After the king's death, there was an awful sense of being in a black hole."[1] She lost her father, of course, and Townsend lost his mentor, friend, and benefactor. The group captain also divorced his wife, Rosemary, shortly after the king's death, leaving an even greater void in his heart.

Margaret quickly shared news of her relationship with her closest confidante, who was now the Queen. Knowing Peter as well as she did, Elizabeth approved of the match, perhaps appreciating the older man's steadying effect on her rather tempestuous sister. The only problem, of course, was the respective status each held: he was a divorced man, and she was a royal. Almost two decades had passed since the abdication crisis ignited by a similar relationship, between Edward VIII and Wallis Simpson, and while this one was markedly different, it was no less troublesome for the Crown.

The Royal Marriages Act of 1772, passed under King George III, required the sovereign's permission for a royal to marry if they wished to remain in the line of succession, which inherently included government approval by the Prime Minister, Cabinet, and Parliament, since Margaret was not yet twenty-five. The act was intended to prevent unsuitable matches that might later be regretted or produce questionable heirs. It did not specifically address the issue of divorce, but if the Royal Family had learned anything from the abdication crisis, they knew that, at the very least, divorce remained controversial in the church. In addition, divorce called into question one's personal character and private morality, the type of scrutiny the Crown could ill afford.

As Head of the Church and Defender of the Faith, Elizabeth was squarely in the crosshairs between a private family matter and a public constitutional dilemma. By all accounts, including her own, the Queen could not endorse the divorced Townsend as her brother-in-law and uphold her duty as sovereign. She herself held no bias against divorced individuals, but she hated the message it sent about the impermanence of marriage, a vow she considered sacrosanct, personally as well as professionally.

This impasse crystallized into a sharp wedge between the two sisters. While their personalities and temperaments had always contrasted, they enjoyed the close bond of relying on each other in the extraordinary circumstances of their father's accession to the throne. Once Elizabeth became the heir presumptive, she could not help being treated differently by others, both inside and outside the palace. Similarly, Margaret, who was then second in line to the throne right behind her sister, could not help feeling less-than.

Numerous sources recount how Princess Margaret would often comment on her unique status as the daughter of a king and sister of a queen, which left her in a kind of royal purgatory, entitled but uncertain about her purpose and ultimate importance compared with family members wearing crowns. The sisters' childhood governess, Marion Crawford, "Crawfie" as she was called, reported that the dutiful Elizabeth often compensated for her destined status by doing more than her share of chores assigned to them. Early on, the future queen wanted to somehow make up for the fact that the crown would land on her instead of her sister.

But by loving Peter Townsend, Margaret forced the Queen to choose between untenable options: disregard her duty and grant permission for the marriage or risk losing her only sibling at a time when they were already growing apart. Presumably, the stakes weren't nearly as high as they had been when the sisters' Uncle David gave up his royal status to be with the woman he loved. Elizabeth was queen, not Margaret, and Townsend was well-bred and well-liked. Nevertheless, for the players in this royal love triangle, no outcome offered a satisfactory solution.

After Margaret confided in her sister, Elizabeth apparently asked that the Princess and Group Captain Townsend keep their relationship private until well after the coronation. Thus, the telltale gesture caught by journalists became the catalyst for a situation that captured headlines and magazines, revealing their personal relationship to the public sooner than preferred. Once it was clear the Queen could not grant her permission, the remaining option, again based on the Royal Marriages Act, was for the romantic couple to wait until after Margaret's twenty-fifth birthday. Presumably, then she would not need her big sister's permission to marry.

Urged by Churchill as well as her private secretary, Alan "Tommy" Lascelles, and others on her staff, Queen Elizabeth agreed to separate the lovers by posting Group Captain Townsend to the British Embassy in Belgium. The consensus was that perhaps, given time, the relationship would dwindle and end on its own. As it turned out, however, the interval became simply another romantic hurdle for the couple to jump. Tabloids urged them on, featuring pictures of the Princess "pining away" or Townsend gazing wistfully into the distance on the streets of Brussels.

By the time Princess Margaret celebrated her twenty-fifth birthday on August 21, 1955, another even larger obstacle loomed, one that promised another delay. Apparently, the Royal Marriages Act contained a second proviso determining that if a royal personage over the age of twenty-five wished to marry, they did not need the sovereign's blessing, but they would need official approval by Parliament, not to be granted before twelve months' time to allow for discussion, debate, and consent in each of the two Houses.

With divorce still highly controversial, particularly among the old establishment, and with so many politicians involved, each wanting to please his own diverse constituency, it was highly unlikely that the Princess and Townsend would receive their government's stamp of approval. Without official consent, Margaret could marry her handsome war hero, a divorced father of two sons, but would be required to relinquish her royal status, including her income, privileges, and titles.

While the dust settled from this revelation, the Queen, as well as the Queen Mother, gave Margaret a wide berth, unwilling to become the recipient of her volatile emotions about the situation. They practiced what's typically called "ostriching" within the Royal Family, which is indeed as it sounds—burying one's head in the sand in hopes of the problem going away. As tempting as it might be to fault Her Majesty, by this point the matter was out of her hands.

She may or may not have known about the second hoop, a veritable closed door as it were, in the Royal Marriages Act. Because of her love and loyalty to her sister, and her relative inexperience as sovereign, it seems feasible that Queen Elizabeth did not know, was not told, or was misinformed about Margaret's ability to marry Townsend. In the "Gloriana" episode of *The Crown*, the Queen is portrayed as almost as frustrated and outraged as her sister when she learns fully of the dilemma.

Once Princess Margaret's will-she-or-won't-she options became clear in the press, pressure mounted for an official statement on her decision and the fate of her relationship with Townsend. What had originally been anticipated as their climactic reunion that fall became instead a kind of showdown with reality. Group Captain Townsend returned to Britain in September ostensibly to attend a military air show, and after several anguished conversations with the Princess, by October they mutually agreed to end their romance.

Many within the palace, both family and staff, suspected that the Princess Royal would never be able to live without the entitled lifestyle that seemed her only consolation prize as the runner-up to the Crown. Ending the relationship with Townsend at least allowed her to save face publicly, with many subjects perceiving her decision as a great personal sacrifice made out of duty to the monarchy and in service to the Commonwealth.

Regardless of Princess Margaret's motives, there can be no doubt that the choice made by her sister, Queen Elizabeth, was quite painful. When forced to navigate matters of the heart using the compass of the Church, Her Majesty upheld her duty while bearing the criticism inflicted by a wounded sister. If the young monarch had not yet fully realized the crushing demands of her role, then dealing with this unexpected situation forced her to consider the depth of her convictions.

While dealing with her sister's engagement with a divorced man was a personal, more private conflict, soon enough Queen Elizabeth confronted overt public criticism in the form of a scathing article written by self-proclaimed monarchist John Grigg, Lord Altrincham. Not two years had passed since Margaret's breakup with Townsend, and the Royal Family was enjoying their annual summer holiday at Balmoral in the Scottish Highlands, when a small periodical called the *National and English Review* published an article titled "The Monarch Today," by Grigg, the magazine's thirty-three-year-old editor.

Grigg possessed an impressive pedigree, educated at Eton and Oxford before becoming an officer in the Grenadier Guards. As a member of the traditionally conservative Tory party, Grigg was nonetheless progressive, being publicly critical of MPs from his own party whom he considered unfit to serve as well as endorsing the ordination of women in the Church of England. Considering his political and social beliefs, it wasn't surprising that Grigg would write something critical about the monarchy. More shocking, however, was the bold, blunt force of his vehement attack.

In his article Grigg directly denounced the upper echelon of royal advisers as "tweedy" and "tight," more intent on preserving the institution of the monarchy as they knew it than allowing it to evolve in step with the times. Most stunning of all, Grigg refused to couch his criticism of Her Majesty in vague, deferential terms. Instead, he referenced her as a "priggish schoolgirl" with "woefully inadequate training" for her role as the sovereign of a modern, twentieth-century United Kingdom. Her speeches received the most criticism, both for lack of substance as well as for the Queen's scripted, pinched delivery, which he called "a pain in the neck."[2]

Grigg tried to offset his bald remarks by offering them only as "loyal and constructive criticism" aimed at helping improve the monarchy before it was too late. But the damage had been done. Like insulting someone else's mother, brazenly criticizing Her Majesty in such a public way was beyond impolite or controversial. It simply wasn't done. Consequently, Grigg became an infamous celebrity for his fifteen minutes of fame, appearing in a television interview with Robin Day and earning an outraged face slap on the street from Mr. Philip K. Burbidge, a retired military man and faithful member of the League of Empire Loyalists.

Dismissed by government leaders and the archbishop of Canterbury as presumptuous and silly, Grigg's remarks resonated within Buckingham Palace like a shrill alarm clock providing the proverbial wake-up call. According to biographer Sally Bedell Smith in *Elizabeth the Queen*, Her Majesty's assistant private secretary at the time, Martin Charteris, as well as her husband, Prince Philip, thought the criticism was worth considering.[3] The Queen's response remains unknown, but Grigg's words likely stung with a ring of truth.

One of Elizabeth's greatest ongoing struggles was already in play: between the old-guard supporters of the historical monarchy and her own instincts on how to fulfill her duties as a modern sovereign in a rapidly changing, post–World War II Commonwealth. In light of Grigg's criticism, she came across as nothing but a monarchial marionette, one who would become increasingly irrelevant, according to Lord Altrincham, as her youth and beauty faded.

With her husband's support and encouragement, the Queen agreed to receive voice coaching from professionals associated with the British Broadcasting Corporation (BBC), including David Attenborough, who the Queen would decades later knight for his work as a renowned natural historian and documentary maker. With their input and much practice, Queen Elizabeth improved "by lowering her voice and smoothing out her clipped accent" but refused to give up the use of scripted speeches.[4]

Staying on script in her public appearances provided a security blanket for the naturally reserved young woman, and it also prevented the kind of spontaneous, off-the-cuff comments that had caused trouble for her Uncle David and her maverick sister. One wonders whether her scripted speeches also pay homage to her father, King George VI, since he too depended on knowing what he would say ahead of the occasion.

To make matters worse, another article soon appeared that enflamed the controversy ignited by Grigg in "The Monarch Today." Journalist and social critic Malcolm Muggeridge published "Does England Really Need a Queen?" in the popular American magazine *The Saturday Evening Post*.

Muggeridge had written a similar article two years prior, "The Royal Soap Opera" in the *New Statesman*, but it was largely ignored at the time because of the coverage of Princess Margaret and Group Captain Peter Townsend. Muggeridge's new challenge was even more pointed. He made his disdain clear and challenged the monarchy, and Her Majesty in particular, for the promotion of antiquated customs that perpetuated the elitist nepotism inherent in the British aristocracy. By maintaining royal privileges at taxpayers' expense, the Royal Family did nothing to benefit anyone other than snobs and sycophants.[5] Muggeridge wrote:

> When, as in the case of Queen Elizabeth II, a monarch only reigns, with no ruling powers whatsoever, it is inevitable that the focus of interest should be transferred from the office to the person.
>
> It is the queen herself, her family, her associates, her way of life, which hold the public attention. The role she has inherited is purely symbolic, and the functions that go with it are purely ceremonial. Because she has no power, she must be, in herself, wondrous. If she were ordinary, she would be nothing.[6]

Muggeridge was villainized even more than John Grigg and almost lost his new job as a BBC correspondent because of his criticism of the Crown. He would go on to become an iconic broadcaster and later experience a dramatic Christian conversion that he described in his bestselling book, *Jesus Rediscovered*. While he remained a social critic, particularly of popular culture, for the rest of his life, Muggeridge, in his roles as apologist and evangelist, also brought considerable attention to the life and ministry of Mother Teresa in his book *Something Beautiful for God*.

Whether Muggeridge's additional complaints added pressure to make royal changes, we will likely never know. In depicting Queen Elizabeth's reaction to Lord Altrincham's critique, *The Crown*'s "Marionettes" episode invents a scene in which the aristocratic editor is discreetly invited to Buckingham Palace to meet with the Queen's private secretary, Martin Charteris, only to be cornered by the Queen herself. Their conversation is tense at first but becomes more relaxed as the Queen, sensing his underlying goodwill, realizes the merit in his suggestions. As they conclude, she tells Grigg that their meeting never happened, a clever hedge planted by scriptwriter Peter Morgan.

Robert Lacey, royal historian and consultant for *The Crown*, said, "Altrincham is an example of the monarchy falling behind. Because ultimately, the monarchy is only as good as the people doing the job. We're very proud in Britain of our system, in distinguishing between the 'executive,' that's the politicians, and the dignified, that's the queen. But sometimes, as we see with Lord Altrincham, that gets out of step."[7]

Whether Her Majesty ever came face-to-face with her constructive critic remains unknown, but it's clear that she quickly accommodated more changes than just voice coaching and new speechwriters. In fact, evidence of change occurred concurrently with the release of Muggeridge's *Saturday Evening Post* article when Queen Elizabeth made a highly anticipated, almost two-week visit to North America, with her time split almost evenly between Canada and the United States.

Shortly after touching down in Ottawa, Queen Elizabeth delivered her first speech to be televised live. She spoke in both English and French, which she learned as a girl and has remained fluent in to this day, and read for the first time from a teleprompter, requiring her to look directly into the camera. Obviously a bit nervous, she nevertheless prefaced her speech by telling millions of live viewers, "I want to talk to you more personally."[8]

This tone and format would be repeated a few months later when the Queen allowed her annual Christmas message to be televised. Although Prince Philip has always been an early adapter of technology, Elizabeth was understandably nervous. "Television is the worst of all, but I suppose when one gets used to it, it is not so terrible as at first sight," she wrote to her prime minister at the time, Anthony Eden.[9]

She would be marking the twenty-fifth anniversary of the first such holiday address, given by her grandfather, King George V, back in 1932. This would be the sixth Christmas broadcast of her reign, and she already held the tradition in high regard because it allowed her the opportunity to speak directly and personally to her subjects without input or approval from Downing Street or Parliament. Now her connection with them would be even more up close and personal.

Prince Philip served more or less as her producer for the historic broadcast, choosing the Long Library at Sandringham, the Queen's private residence in Norfolk, as her setting. Two cameras, both with a teleprompter, were used, while the microphone remained hidden by a holiday arrangement of evergreen and holly. After a slow pan of the exterior of

Sandringham, the camera closed in on one window, presumably with Her Majesty inside, before cutting to her as she sat at a small desk. Holiday cards and framed family photos imbued warmth and cheer to the black-and-white broadcast.

Her Majesty's delivery was flawless, still slightly tentative as she warmed up to the opportunity yet polished enough to

convey confidence. She began by celebrating the ability to invite viewers into her home even as she could visit theirs thanks to technology, saying, "I very much hope that this new medium will make my Christmas message more personal and direct."[10] She then wisely took the opportunity to address the essence of change embodied by television: "That it is possible for some of you to see me today is just another example of the speed at which things are changing all around

Queen Elizabeth seated at her desk after giving her first televised address, Christmas Day, 1957.
Daily Mail/Shutterstock

us. Because of these changes I am not surprised that many people feel lost and unable to decide what to hold on to and what to discard. How to take advantage of the new life without losing the best of the old."[11]

Many historians and royal experts agree that the British monarchy should have gone the way of the red phone boxes, console televisions, and vinyl records—existing only as sentimental reminders of bygone days and useful only for conjuring up nostalgia. A few might even claim that that is indeed what the monarchy *has* become. But even a cursory look at Queen Elizabeth II's reign would quickly provide evidence to the contrary.

Placed squarely in the middle between her sister and her duty as Head of the Church, Her Majesty tried her best to indulge Princess Margaret while upholding her own duty as sovereign. The result, in hindsight, appears to have been a costly battle with no clear winners—except future generations of Royals, including Prince Charles, his mother's successor. For he, along with two of his siblings and his son Prince Harry, arguably benefited from the lessons learned during Princess Margaret's romance with Group Captain Townsend.

While the Queen's own views on divorce likely haven't wavered, changes in culture and society have necessitated changes in the institutions of both church and state. The Royal Marriages Act of 1772 was finally repealed by the Perth Agreement of 2011; however, the sovereign's right to veto any marriage in the direct line of succession was not clarified until the Succession to the Crown Act of 2013. Officially, the sovereign must grant permission to marry for the first six people in the line of royal succession. Other members of the Royal Family do not officially require the reigning monarch's approval in order to wed. The Succession to the Crown Act also replaced the centuries-held practice of preferring male primogeniture with absolute primogeniture, meaning eldest children, regardless of their gender, would precede their siblings, including brothers, in line to the throne.

Her willingness to learn from personally painful conflicts

has influenced her ability to help others embrace changes they might otherwise reject. Perhaps we see this most clearly in how Her Majesty has served the Commonwealth. It could have easily become an outdated club of remnant imperialism, but instead it transformed into a sophisticated, diplomatic alliance representing a full spectrum of countries and cultures because Queen Elizabeth created a role for her brand of strong, gentle leadership that didn't exist before. The Commonwealth thrives because of the combination of the Queen's hard work, including the grueling demands of traveling weeks and months each year to visit most all of the six to seven dozen members of the Commonwealth, and her personal engagement with both individuals and their cultures.

Regardless of the political view one holds about the United Kingdom and the Commonwealth, no one can deny the indelible stamp of stability, dignity, and compassion left on them by Queen Elizabeth II.

Acknowledging the Queen's influence on British history doesn't mean the monarchy no longer has detractors. During my time in the UK, I discovered that while nearly everyone loves Her Majesty, many don't like the monarchy or support a vision for it going forward. They consider Queen Elizabeth II one of a kind and worry that her successors will not be able to sustain the legacy they inherit from her. One person holding this mixed view was a young Irishman who I met on a train heading northwest from London and terminating in Manchester.

Leaving the city to visit my friends Andy and Heather

Pratt in Preston, I took a Virgin Atlantic train out of Euston Station. I had reserved a seat on an early afternoon train, hoping to avoid the crush of weekend travelers later on that Friday. Apparently, however, the rush had already started, and I had not reserved a seat after all—and even if I had, I wasn't about to ask the elderly woman clutching her hand luggage in seat 17A to get up. Plus, elbow-to-elbow passengers overflowing in the noisy carriage made me feel a bit claustrophobic.

People crowded the aisle both in front of and behind me as I tried to swim upstream to the next train car. It too proved to be packed, as did the next one behind it. Finally, as we left the station, I paused in the small space—containing an exit and luggage bins—between two carriages. I would have to stand, but the journey was under two hours, and the inconvenience of standing seemed a small price to pay for peace and quiet. An attendant came through and scanned my ticket and offered to help find me a seat, which I appreciated but declined.

After enjoying a half hour of watching the London suburbs give way to rolling pastures, now a sun-faded green after being mown for hay, and a sprinkling of farmhouses and villages, I shot a sixty-second video of the English countryside going by to send to family and friends. Several people had passed through my little passageway en route to a bathroom or the café two cars down, but then after a quick stop at Rugby, a young man wandered in and decided to join me. In his midtwenties, he was dressed in canvas work pants, boots, and a hoodie, looking like a trade worker who had just come from a job site.

"D' you mind, sir?" he asked, dropping his backpack and

kit bag a few feet away and leaning against the closed exit door. "I had a seat but gave 't up to a lady just boarded—could've been my gram, I reckon."

"No worries," I said. "A lot less crowded here. Good of you to give her your seat."

He shrugged, took out his phone, and texted while I resumed watching the world go by. After a few minutes, I decided to stretch my legs in the direction of the café. "Would you mind watching my bag?" I asked the young man. "Just for a minute?"

"'Course," he said.

"Grabbing a coffee," I said. "Can I get you one?"

"No thanks, mate," he said. "Cheers, though."

When I returned ten minutes later with my flat white, he looked up and nodded. "Still here." I thanked him and asked whether he was going all the way to Manchester.

"Yeah," he smiled. "Goin' home. You're from the States, right? What part?"

After we exchanged names and made small talk, Sean informed me that he worked for a large construction company. He mostly installed commercial kitchens and had a knack for fitting countertops. His supervisor had assigned him to train a crew in London for a few weeks, so now he was "extra chuffed" to go home on weekends to see his kids. His face lit up as he described his young daughter and infant son, pulling up their happy faces on his phone.

Eventually, our chat turned to my work and the reason for my visit. When I mentioned the Queen, I sensed Sean was not a fan, which was confirmed as he hesitated before saying, "Grew up in Belfast, so most folk . . . we didn't think much of the Queen. You'll have heard of the Troubles, yeah?"

"Right," I said. "And what do you think now that you're here working?"

Sean folded his arms and sighed, ignoring a beep from his phone. "Well, my mind's changed a wee bit. Our politics aside, I think she's quite decent, actually. Don't have much use for her family and the way our tax supports 'em all. But at least she makes them work a bit, charities and all." The lilt and speed of his voice forced me to process his message. "Hope that doesn't offend you, mate." I realized he had interpreted my translation delay as a response to his opinion.

"Not at all," I said. "If you don't mind my asking, what has changed your mind about the Queen?"

"I'm not sure," he said and became visibly emotional. "Being a dad, I think. This world . . . frightens me for me kids. No certainty . . . no morals left. Not much to build on. But the Queen . . . she tries to do what's right and all. She reminds me of me granny and pops—they'd spin in their graves if they heard me!" He chuckled. "Just *caring* about people, just being *kind* like, you know? Can't right explain it—" His voice choked, and he wiped his eyes with his hand. "Sorry, mate."

"Not a problem. Thank you for sharing that, Sean."

An automated voice announced our arrival into Preston, my stop. I wished him a good weekend with his kids and thanked him again for talking with me. He extended his hand and we shook. Just as the train glided to a stop and the exit door exhaled open before the platform, I turned back to him and said, "You're a good man. And I can tell you're a *great* dad! I bet your grandparents—and even the Queen herself—would be proud of you."

*Change is a constant; managing it has
become an expanding discipline. The way
we embrace it defines our future.*

—*Golden Jubilee address
before Parliament,
2002*

chapter five

TIME *and* TIDE

KEEPING CALM AND CARRYING ON

While we might assume that someone with as much wealth and privilege as Queen Elizabeth never worries about what the future holds, Her Majesty is just as human as any of us. From her most remarkable vantage point on national and world affairs, Her Majesty has likely witnessed more global changes in every facet of human life than any of her royal predecessors. From the moon landing to microchips, from color television to all-cable access, from bombs to birth control, from socialism to social media, the Queen has experienced an astounding array of advancements, inventions, innovations, and shifts in culture.

As she indicated in a speech before both Houses of Parliament during her Golden Jubilee in 2002, change has, in fact, been a defining characteristic of her reign:

Since 1952 I have witnessed the transformation of the international landscape through which this country must chart its course, the emergence of the Common-wealth, the growth of the European Union, the end of the Cold War, and now the dark threat of international terrorism. This has been matched by no less rapid developments at home, in the devolved shape of our nation, in the structure of society, in technology and communications, in our work and in the way we live.[1]

Concluding that the way we embrace change defines our future, the Queen implicitly revealed the role faith plays. Accepting change, especially that brought by loss, requires faith if one is to relinquish fear of uncertainty and rely on God's unchanging providence. The Bible assures us, "Jesus Christ is the same yesterday and today and forever" (Hebrews 13:8). Queen Elizabeth has learned that regardless of what circumstances bring or what changes occur, her steadfast faith in God will sustain her.

While Her Majesty famously described 1992 as her *"annus horribilis"* due to three of her four children's marriages ending in very public divorces along with a major fire at Windsor Castle, five years later she endured another watershed season with lessons on change and the pains of loss. The summer of 1997 proved to be a turning point for how she fulfilled her duties as Queen, along with the relationship between the monarchy and the public.

Prior to that summer, Her Majesty had turned seventy-one in April, which she had celebrated quietly at Windsor Castle by lunching with the Queen Mother (then ninety-six) in the garden at Frogmore Cottage. Less than two weeks later, back at Buckingham Palace, the Queen welcomed her tenth prime minister, Tony Blair, the landslide-winning Labour Party leader, for the first of their weekly chats. This meeting is depicted at the beginning of the film *The Queen* as a study in contrasts: old and new, monarch and republican, conservative and liberal, tradition and progress. In his memoir, Blair would later describe how that first meeting gave him a sense of his "relative seniority, or lack of it, in the broad sweep of history."[2]

One of Blair's primary tasks for his first months in office included overseeing the handover of Hong Kong—a British colony for over a century—to China. Set in motion years earlier by Margaret Thatcher amid a thorny web of political and economic stakeholders, the peaceful transfer signaled the end of the British Empire, an unraveling that started shortly before Queen Elizabeth's accession with the independence of India. In fact, that summer marked the fiftieth anniversary of that momentous change, bringing "an emotive reminder of how the empire was supposed to end" versus the "rude truth of how rancorously it is in fact ending."[3]

Her Majesty sent Prince Charles to represent the Crown at the ceremony of transfer on July 1, 1997 in Hong Kong, where he read a glass-half-full speech on her behalf. Largely overlooked amid the cultural, political, and historical crosscurrents was the fact that the Prince of Wales traveled there by means of the Royal Yacht, *Britannia*, on what would be its final official voyage, yet another tangible reminder of the significant changes taking place in the monarchy. It was another symbol of the shifting, shrinking power of a monarchy that was once the world's most powerful.

Giving up *Britannia* was likely one of the most personally painful losses for Her Majesty, certainly as a material possession. Considering both the innumerable privileges she enjoys as well as her life's many devastating sorrows, surrendering the royal yacht reflects a unique kind of loss. Even pairing "royal yacht" with "loss" would seem to be an oxymoron, representing the knotty issues of cost, entitlement, and public perception that led to the vessel's release and decommissioning.

Unlike the usual associations one might have with the possession of a yacht—wealth, privilege, status—*Britannia* was the last in a long, historical tradition beginning in 1660 with King Charles II. As the eighty-third official seafaring vessel of the British monarch, the *Britannia* had been commissioned by Elizabeth's father, George VI, who sadly didn't live to see its completion. As was fitting for a twentieth-century vessel, the new royal yacht was designed for complete ocean-going voyages, serving as a kind of floating palace for the Queen and Royal Family. It was also crafted to serve as a hospital ship during wartime as well as a shelter for Her Majesty and Prince Philip in the event of a nuclear attack, neither of which has been needed, fortunately.

On its maiden voyage the year after the Queen's coronation, the *Britannia* sailed from Portsmouth to Malta, an eight-day trip bringing young Prince Charles and Princess Anne to their parents at the end of their months-long Commonwealth Tour. Over the next forty-four years, the royal yacht would log more than a million nautical miles, roughly the equivalent of sailing around the world once a year. She would visit dignitaries on almost seven hundred foreign visits, port in 135 countries, and drop anchor on nearly three hundred official functions throughout the British Isles.

Britannia hosted US presidents, from Eisenhower to Clinton, and served as honeymoon headquarters for at least four royal couples, most famously Charles and Diana in 1981. In fact, the ship's honeymoon suite is the only accommodation with a double bed! The ship sailed the just-opened Saint Lawrence Seaway to Chicago, docking there to make history. The royal yacht also evacuated over a thousand refugees during the civil war in Yemen in 1986.

In the election leading to Labour's victory and Blair's term as prime minister, Conservative party candidates committed to replacing *Britannia* with a more cost-efficient model, its maintenance budget already slashed in years prior. Labour leaders remained mum on their proposed plans for the ship until after they won the general election, when they immediately announced plans to retire the vessel without a replacement, which was deemed too costly. During times of economic struggle, public criticism often aimed at the royal yacht as an easy target. Critics complained that the *Britannia* was only an expensive toy for which commoners were forced to pay. This claim wasn't entirely true because the royal yacht, in addition to providing transportation and hosting official state functions, also attracted foreign businesses and investors to meetings called "Sea Days." The Overseas Trade Board estimated that these events yielded about three billion pounds (about four billion US dollars) between 1991 and 1995 alone.[4]

Nevertheless, because of public criticism as well as the increasing upkeep and maintenance costs, the *Britannia* made its last official voyage in midsummer of 1997, ferrying Prince Charles and political leaders to and from Hong Kong. Somehow it seemed oddly fitting and all the sadder that this naval emblem of the monarchy ended its service with a final goodbye to another lost part of the British Empire.

A few months later, as part of their annual summer holiday at Balmoral, the Queen's Scottish estate, the Royal Family enjoyed one last ride on the ship that had been a shelter for them. Prince Andrew and his daughters were on board, along with Princess Anne with her two children and her second husband, Timothy Laurence. Prince Edward brought along his girlfriend, Sophie Rhys-Jones, whom he would marry two years later in 1999. Princess Margaret could not sail, but both her daughter, Sarah Chatto, and son, David Linley, along with their respective spouses, enjoyed one last voyage.

They sailed along the coast, making their usual stop at the Castle of Mey, the Queen Mother's personal retreat. The mood was understandably melancholy. *Britannia* represented more than just luxury on the open seas. As public scrutiny and media attention had increased over the years, the need for privacy and places immune from the telephoto lenses of paparazzi grew as well. *Britannia* provided that kind of escape.

In William Kuhn's insightful novel *Mrs. Queen Takes the Train*, the character of Queen Elizabeth suffers from depression as she ages and confronts her mortality, feeling that she has missed out on the joy of living a "normal" life. The novel fictionalizes a fascinating scenario and relies on factual details, both historical and descriptive, to make "Mrs. Queen" a lovable character with whom we identify. When Her Majesty decides to enjoy a runaway holiday off-duty from her royal responsibilities, she heads to Edinburgh (via the train of the book's title) to see *Britannia*, permanently docked there as a tourist attraction, one last time. Arriving after hours, she passes as a cleaning lady and enjoys reminiscing about the many moments and milestones enjoyed on the ship. "I have been happy here," she realizes, quite poignantly.[5]

Her Majesty the Queen wipes away a tear at the decommissioning ceremony for the Royal Yacht *Britannia*, December 11, 1997.
Tim Graham/Getty Images

Perhaps that sense of happiness enjoyed on the decks of *Britannia* explains the tears shed by Queen Elizabeth and other members of the Royal Family when the royal yacht was officially decommissioned in a ceremony four months after their last cruise up the coast. Held in December on a dreary, blustery day in Portsmouth, the solemn event concluded with the Band of the Royal Marines playing "Highland Cathedral" on bagpipes. Clocks on the ship were all stopped at 15:01, the time when Her Majesty had departed the royal yacht for the last time.[6]

Yes, she had been happy there.

In between that last voyage up the Scottish coast to Balmoral in August and the royal yacht's decommissioning ceremony in December, a far greater and more devastating loss occurred. Queen Elizabeth and Prince Philip were still on summer holiday in Scotland, along with Prince Charles and his two young sons, Prince William and Prince Harry, when the boys' mother, Princess Diana, suffered fatal injuries in a car crash in a motorway tunnel in Paris.

By this time Charles and Diana had been officially divorced for just over a year after a four-year separation. Their romance, wedding, tumultuous marriage, and subsequent divorce had created a frenzy of public interest—"the soapy glamour of beautifully groomed young people doing expensive things"[7] as the *Guardian* once called it. And it was not only the British public devouring details of the next generation of royals; the fascination of Americans, Australians, and Europeans had turned Charles and Diana's relationship into an international saga.

In many ways, royal reality delivered more salacious intrigue than any romance novel. Beginning like a fairy tale with a royal wedding that Cinderella would envy, the relationship between Queen Elizabeth's eldest son, the heir apparent to the throne, and Princess Diana ended like a soap opera. By the time their divorce was finalized, the tawdry details behind the collapse of their marriage had been exposed, complete with he-said/she-said volleys back and forth about such topics as adultery, bulimia, depression, and deception.

By the time Charles and Diana finally divorced, most royal insiders considered it a relief. Reconciliation had moved from unlikely to impossible, and in June 1996 Queen Elizabeth herself urged the pair to end their legal union. After agreement had been reached concerning terms of settlement two months later, Diana emerged more popular than ever. She had relinquished the title of Her Royal Highness along with any future claim to the British throne but had retained her title as Princess of Wales. In addition to the generous cash settlement, an annual allowance, and her apartments at Kensington Palace, Diana had won the hearts of millions of devoted fans.

Princess Diana's unique combination of innocence, youth, beauty, and shyness had brought a breath of fresh air into the stuffy traditionalism of the historical monarchy. She not only had her own royal style and star quality, she also possessed the ability to show people she cared. Frequently breaking with protocol or precedential tradition, Diana wasn't afraid to show emotion, hug children, pause to talk with guests, or take up a neglected cause. During the year after her divorce, the Princess basked in the full spotlight of her celebrity, carving out a distinct royal role for herself unlike any other.

Even as she continued supporting charities, raising funds for worthwhile causes around the world, and, by everyone's account, being a wonderfully engaged mother to her two sons, Princess Diana struggled to find love and stability in her private life. Her frequent dates and sporadic relationships made tabloid headlines and brought increased media scrutiny. Diana was both a princess to which her followers could aspire while remaining a person who was grounded, accessible, and authentic. Her life, seemingly perfect in so many ways, had fractured and then crumbled, only to be rebuilt by her sheer will, charming personality, and radiant smile.

This newfound status as the "People's Princess" made her premature death all the more dramatic for her legion of fans, tragic for those who knew her, and sensational for the paparazzi whose dogged pursuit contributed to her demise. At the time of her death, Diana had been involved with Dodi Fayed, the son of Egyptian business tycoon Mohamed al-Fayed, whose holdings at the time included Harrods, the iconic London department store.

Dodi was known for being an extravagant playboy and showered Diana with attention, exotic gifts, and romantic vacations, often at luxury locations owned by his wealthy father. Their budding romance had emerged in the press less than a month earlier, complete with sexy photos and lurid details. Inside the Royal Family, it was merely another episode in the whirlwind escapades of the newly divorced Di. Her sons, then fifteen and twelve, were quietly embarrassed by her ongoing infatuation with "bad boys" as played out in the tabloid media.

When the British embassy in Paris called the Queen's assistant private secretary, Robin Janvrin, to inform him of the accident and the Princess's injuries, it was nearly one o'clock in the morning. Three hours later another call was made to inform them that Princess Diana had died, along with her companion Dodi Fayed and Henri Paul, the driver of the black Mercedes S280. Only the Princess's bodyguard, Trevor Rees-Jones, survived the crash in the tunnel beneath Pont de l'Alma. Like the most elite of iconic superstars, Princess Diana died at the zenith of her fame, immortalized by her own indefatigable commitment to be a different kind of royal.

Queen Elizabeth's response to her former daughter-in-law's death has received considerable criticism and scrutiny, particularly as portrayed in the film *The Queen*. Many critics complained that she was cool, aloof, withdrawn, even vengeful now that the woman who had caused so many problems for the palace was no longer alive. Yet in hindsight, the way Her Majesty initially handled the tragic loss of her grandsons' mother fits with who she is, both as queen and as a grandmother, as she would later comment when she finally delivered a televised address prior to Diana's funeral.

The Queen relied on her instinctive resistance to the kind of blatant emotional transparency Diana had used as currency during the previous five years. Reinforced by her staff and institutional advisers, Her Majesty's response was formal, polite, discreet, and private. Foremost, she was concerned about the welfare of her grandsons. Only through the prodding of new Prime Minister Tony Blair and the swelling grief of the British public did Queen Elizabeth realize that this was indeed a watershed occasion. It was not only the death of the People's Princess, as Blair christened Diana in his stopgap remarks prior to the Queen's address, it was also a transformational turning point for the essence of the monarchy, requiring it to adapt or sever itself from the subjects it is committed to serve.

The great irony is that through her death Diana became the catalyst for a royal renaissance within the monarchy. In her life she proved to be fresh, contemporary, relatable, easily the most popular member of the Royal Family, perhaps even more beloved than the Queen herself. Through the battles of her media war with Prince Charles, Diana had already proven herself to be savvy, shrewd, and strategic. She knew how to manipulate public opinion even as she grew increasingly claustrophobic as the walls of paparazzi continued closing in around her.

The revelations of her Andrew Morton biography, *Diana: Her True Story*, in 1992 allowed her to tell her side of the story, the way she wanted to tell it, without the censorious filter of the palace. When the book launched, it was assumed to be a young journalist making a name for himself by seizing an opportunity to feed the growing interest in the Princess. As its claims came under scrutiny, it became apparent that Diana had met with Morton numerous times to contribute material as well as provide her covert consent, which Morton confirmed with evidence five years later after Diana's death.

With the book's serialization and publication, rumors of their disastrous marriage, compounded by Charles's infidelity with Camilla Parker Bowles, had basis in fact. Diana emerged as an emotionally warm and caring young woman trying to cope with a loveless marriage in an archaic, institution-bound, detached family. She revealed her ongoing battle with depression, along with at least two suicide attempts, compounded by bulimia. Suddenly, the veil on royal life had not been lifted but torn asunder.

Two years later Prince Charles went one step further by participating in an authorized biography, *The Prince of Wales*, by respected journalist Jonathan Dimbleby. While acknowledging his infidelity, the Prince portrays Diana as a fragile, neurotic, unstable young woman who couldn't handle the pressures of royal life. To put a fine point on his revelations, Prince Charles participated in an interview with Dimbleby, reiterating the book's claims. Returning the volley, Diana gave an interview on the BBC television program *Panorama* the following year, offering a dramatic, sympathetic rebuttal to Charles's allegations. The result was that "the world divided into two camps: those who sided with the Princess of Wales, who included many feminists and constitutional reformers, identifying her with the plight of oppressed women, or with a modernist critique of the Monarchy—and supporters of the Prince."[8]

In many ways, Princess Diana's death brought to a head the excruciating exposure endured by the Royal Family in 1992. That horrible year had been a catastrophic chain of calamity, mostly fueled by the tawdry revelations of her children's personal lives. Between the sexual and romantic escapades of Sarah Ferguson, the Duchess of York and wife of Prince Andrew, and the antics of Charles and Diana, including the publication of the Morton biography on the Princess, the palace endured nothing short of humiliation.

On the heels of photos showing Fergie on a Mediterranean holiday with Texas oilman Steve Wyatt, the Duke and Duchess of York announced their separation in March.

Later that year, another round of picture-perfect tabloid shots would reveal Fergie in totally compromising positions with her financial adviser, John Bryan.

While not as explicitly embarrassing as revelations about the Yorks and the Waleses, in April it was announced that Princess Anne and her husband, Captain Mark Phillips, were divorcing after eighteen years of marriage. It would later be revealed that Phillips had not only been unfaithful with a woman in New Zealand but had also fathered a child by her.

On top of the constant PR explosions ignited by her children and their partners, the Queen faced the ordeal of an actual fire at Windsor Castle, her favorite of royal residences, that November. A curtain in the Queen's Private Chapel caught fire from a spotlight pressed against it and spread from there. While no serious injuries or deaths resulted, almost one hundred rooms suffered major damage. Most works of art and antiques from the Royal Collection were saved, either retrieved or on loan for exhibitions, but a few were lost. Estimated costs of repairs soared to over £30 million, with PM John Major recommending that taxpayers foot the bill.

This additional public monetary burden was not received well and stirred up long-standing debates on the tax-exempt status of Her Majesty and the Royal Family. Many members of Parliament complained that the Queen, one of the world's wealthiest individuals who at the time paid no income tax, should cover at least part of the repair costs. A kind of compromise was reached, with Windsor opened for more extensive, and expensive, tours to cover costs, which would eventually total more than $40 million. In addition, the cost conversations sparked by the Windsor fire soon led to dramatic changes, with Queen Elizabeth and

Prince Charles "volunteering" to pay personal income tax, while allowing closer parliamentary budget oversight. The Queen also agreed to pay for the majority of her family's personal expenses from her own income, generated largely by investments and landholdings.

Less than a month after the fire at Her Majesty's favorite home, she gave a speech intended to commemorate the fortieth anniversary of her accession to the throne. With her horrible year nearly behind her, the Queen wondered aloud how "future generations would judge the events of this tumultuous year," adding her hope that hindsight would provide both perspective and compassion. She also acknowledged that criticism comes with her role and that it can be constructive:

> There can be no doubt, of course, that criticism is good for people and institutions that are part of public life. No institution—City, Monarchy, whatever—should expect to be free from the scrutiny of those who give it their loyalty and support, not to mention those who don't. But we are all part of the same fabric of our national society and that scrutiny, by one part or another, can be just as effective if it is made with a touch of gentleness, good humour and understanding. This sort of questioning can also act, and it should do so, as an effective engine for change.[9]

These same observations could also refer to the Queen's initial response to the loss of Princess Diana. Both in her life and in her death, Diana defied precedent. If the Queen had maintained historical precedent and rigid institutional rules, then it would have been at the expense of engaging the enormous outpouring of public grief at the Princess's passing. Her Majesty might have won the battle at the expense of losing the war. Similar to the Pharisees who rebuked Jesus for allowing his disciples to pick and eat grain on the Sabbath (Mark 2:23–28), she could have upheld the letter of the law—precedent and tradition—but instead chose to focus on the spirit of the law, servant-leadership.

After the death of Princess Diana, Queen Elizabeth discovered there were no winners at such a tragic turning point. The only thing to do, as she had pointed out five years earlier, was to embrace change as an opportunity to learn and grow wiser. This was reflected in her annual Christmas speech that year, when the Queen shared how a "sad event," the death of well-known philanthropist Leonard Cheshire, inspired her to persevere by showing "kindness in another's trouble, courage in one's own,"[10] a line from nineteenth-century Australian poet Adam Lindsay Gordon.

Her Majesty Queen Elizabeth II continues to embody both kindness and courage in her response to life's many changes. Bridging two centuries, she inspires generation after generation of her subjects and admirers through her ability to grow, adapt, learn, and share. At the end of 2002, the Queen had endured another painful year of losses with the deaths of both her mother and sister. In her annual Christmas address that year, she revealed the secret to her calm stability: "I know just how much I rely on my own faith to guide me through the good times and the bad. Each day is a new beginning.

I know that the only way to live my life is to try to do what is right, to take the long view, to give of my best in all that the day brings, and to put my trust in God."[11]

Knowing the Bible as well as she does, Her Majesty likely had a favorite passage in mind, one that speaks to both the constancy of life's changes along with the security of God's presence:

> The steadfast love of the LORD never ceases;
>> his mercies never come to an end;
> they are new every morning;
>> great is your faithfulness.
>
> *Lamentations 3:22–23 ESV*

"Did you say the Queen's *faith*? Excuse me, but I couldn't help but overhear your conversation with the research librarian," said a low feminine voice in a stately British accent, the kind I had grown accustomed to hearing from BBC reporters on my hotel telly. I was on my way back to the table that had become my makeshift desk in lieu of using a reading room. Most of my research had already been conducted online, and my visit to the British Library was as much about sheer pleasure as work, as this exchange quickly showed.

Turning to respond to the speaker, I was met by the smiling face of an older woman with short silver hair whose remarkable resemblance to actress Judi Dench stopped me in my tracks. She wore dark slacks and what looked like a man's blue oxford-cloth dress shirt, untucked, with a colorful plaid scarf—Burberry perhaps—tied at the neck. "Is it true you're writing a book about the faith of Her Majesty Queen Elizabeth II?" I could've sworn she performed a subtle little curtsy as she spoke the monarch's name. "Not that it's any of my business—"

"Hello," I said. "Yes, you heard correctly—I'm here conducting research for a book on Her Majesty's personal faith." I introduced myself and offered my hand as politely as possible, which she gently shook as she proclaimed, "Brilliant! What a marvelous idea!" She shifted a threadbare book bag from one hand to the other, and we introduced ourselves. "I met her once, you know, the Queen."

"How wonderful," I said. "Did you get to speak to her? What was she like?"

"No, not really," my look-alike Judi said. "It was one of those official receptions. My son—he's a military veteran—invited me to accompany him as his plus-one. Quite the do it was!"

At this point I asked my new friend whether we might continue our chat over tea or coffee in the King's Library Café on the first floor. She seemed delighted with my offer, and minutes later we were enjoying a cuppa and sticky-toffee glazed gingerbread. Judi was keen to share her thoughts on the Queen as well as highlights from her life. Now a widow about to turn eighty, she had two children, two grandchildren, and two great-grandchildren. "Two by two by two. It's rather like Noah's ark at my flat come the holidays!" she chuckled.

Judi had lived most of her life in Dulwich, a picturesque village just a few miles south of London. After her husband passed away, she moved in with her daughter and grandson in Brixton. She served on her church's women's fellowship committee and volunteered for numerous charities, including her local Oxfam shop, and visited the British Library—"Isn't all this just *grand*?"—at least once a week.

"I've grown up just a few years behind Her Majesty the Queen. I remember watching her coronation when I was probably around twelve or thirteen. She looked so beautiful—that dress with the train! And all those ladies-in-waiting. I used to dream about what that would be like to be one of them, like Cinderella at the ball."

"Amazing," I said, spooning another bite of gingerbread. "How do you think Her Majesty has been able to endure so many dramatic changes throughout her reign?"

"Publicly or privately?" Judi asked before answering both. "Her temperament, composure, and calmness have served her well. She has seen so much change in the world. When you live to our age, nothing surprises one anymore. Moon landings, terrorism—the Troubles in Ireland, I'm thinking, the internet, seeing a dozen PMs, plus all her children and their sad marriages. And losing her sweet mum. . . . It simply boggles my wee mind!"

She laughed then, in a beautiful, unselfconscious way that reminded me of tiny bells ringing. "You're wise to look at Her Majesty's faith—because that's her secret, isn't it? It has to be! I don't know how anyone can survive this life without faith in the providence of God."

*When life seems hard, the courageous
do not lie down and accept defeat;
instead, they are all the more determined
to struggle for a better future.*

*—annual Christmas broadcast,
2008*

chapter six

GRACE *and* GRIT

DANCING WITH DANGER
WHEN NECESSARY

*I*magine waking up in your bedroom one summer morning with sunlight cutting through the drapes, only to look up and see a strange man sitting on the end of your bed. Wearing a dirty T-shirt and faded jeans, he holds half a broken ashtray, which explains the rather nasty cut on his other hand dripping blood onto your bed linens. You jump out of bed, grab for your dressing gown, and shriek, "Get out!" When the intruder ignores your demand, you calmly put on your glasses, pick up the phone on the bedside table, and ask the operator who answers to fetch the police.

The man, a bloke of Irish descent in his early thirties named Michael Fagan, wants to talk about his broken heart because apparently his wife has just left him. Seconds seem like hours as you maintain composure and discreetly push the console button that summons your chambermaid. *Where are the police? Where is the maid? Anyone?*

"Do you have any children?" you ask in order to distract this rather wild-looking young man. His demeanor doesn't frighten you as much as alarm you. If he were going to harm you, surely he would have done it by now. He seems to vacillate between tearful despair and nervous excitement. Something about him reminds you of a wounded bird, a grouse perhaps, with a broken wing.

"Four, is it?" you respond. "Boys? Girls? Yes, I have four as well."

He asks for a smoke, which you use as another opportunity to call the police. You get the same well-spoken operator, who, you hope, hears the urgency in your voice this time. "Yes, ma'am," she assures you. "I'll ring them once more."

Mr. Fagan continues blathering on a bit about his children and his desire for a cigarette. *This is just like my walkabout chats*, you think. By this time, you suspect he must be mentally ill. You're not sure what alarms you more: his presence in your bedroom or that ten minutes have now passed without anyone responding to your calls.

As if reading your thoughts, someone gently opens the door from the hallway, one of the chambermaids. *Anna? Daphne?* She's newish, and you can't recall her name at the moment, but it doesn't matter. *Of course—her name is Elizabeth!* You watch as the young woman assesses the scene and swears. "What's he doing in there?" she cries.[1]

Before you can say a word, she turns on her heel and cries out for the footman, apparently nearby or across the hall. Surely this strange ordeal will end soon. You hear the padded patter of many canine feet and the low, soothing voice of the footman, who has been out walking your beloved corgis.

"Do you think I might have a drink, Your Majesty?"

Mr. Fagan asks. "Or that smoke?" What would normally seem a preposterous idea suddenly appeals to you as well.

The maid says something unintelligible but clearly hysterical. The dogs begin barking ferociously, and all hell breaks loose. The footman, a young man whose face reminds you of your oldest grandson's, enters calmly and, without missing a beat, says, "I can get you that drink, mate—come with me."

Ah, at last, someone with quick wits and a cool head about him. "They're on their way, ma'am," he says, conveying his knowledge of your predicament with his eyes. As you quiet the pups, he leads Mr. Fagan out of the room to the drinks closet, chatting away with him as if they'd just met at their local pub instead of your private bedroom. You begin ushering the dogs into the sitting area and hear voices—police, at last—and a bit of commotion. One never knows what a day might hold. What was it Christ said? "Take therefore no thought for the morrow: for the morrow shall take thought for the things of itself. Sufficient unto the day is the evil thereof" (Matthew 6:34 KJV).

Each day does indeed have enough trouble of its own, even for Her Majesty Queen Elizabeth II.

This fictionalized account is based on known facts of the incident that occurred July 9, 1982, when Michael Fagan startled the awakening Queen with his presence. As it turned out, this was Fagan's second breach of security at Buckingham Palace, having climbed the fourteen-foot stone wall topped with metal spikes and the kind of barbed wire used by many prisons. On his first visit, about a month earlier, Fagan then climbed up a drainpipe and into an unlocked window, where a startled housemaid screamed and called security. Palace guards searched the maid's room but, finding nothing, dismissed her alarm as the result of a bad dream.

Meanwhile, Fagan wandered about as if in a private museum, studying the many historical portraits of the Queen's ancestors and predecessors. He found the throne room where he sat to rest for a while and take in more of the royal art collection displayed. Years later, Fagan told a reporter, "It was like Goldilocks and the Three Bears; I tried one throne and was like 'this one's too soft.' I was having a laugh to myself because there was one right next to it, so I tried another."[2]

Then he proceeded down a hallway and noticed doors with family members' names, including "Charles's Room" and "Diana's Room." By this time, according to Fagan, he needed to relieve himself but could not find a bathroom despite opening numerous doors. Eventually he used a storage pantry full of dog food for the Queen's corgis. In another room, he found a bar table and helped himself to cheese and crackers and half a bottle of red wine. Eventually, he decided to leave and exited through a door leading into the back gardens, where he once again scaled the wall. "It was harder to get out than get in," he later recalled.[3]

Distressed by the breakup with his wife, Fagan spent a sleepless night before returning around 6 a.m. to breach the palace walls for the second time within a month. An off-duty police officer happened to see Fagan climbing the wall and called it in, but palace guards found no sign of an intruder when notified. Fagan strolled along the south side of the palace before turning the corner to the side facing west, where he found an open window and crawled in. He entered the holding room for the stamp collection, valued at over £20 million, curated by the Queen's grandfather, King George V. The door from that room into the palace was locked, so Fagan retreated out the window again, returned the way he had come, and climbed up a drainpipe on the east side. He had unknowingly tripped an alarm upon entering and exiting the stamp room, but the guard on duty at the police substation on palace grounds assumed it was a mechanical error and reset it both times.

Perhaps most ironically of all in this comedy of errors, Fagan next entered through an unlocked window into the office of the master of the household, a position that includes overseeing palace security, then held by Vice-Admiral Sir Peter Ashmore. Fagan then resumed his palace tour of royal art and artifacts, including a crystal ashtray that his nervous hands could not contain. Taking the jagged remains with him, the Irishman promptly cut his hand and left a trail that led into Her Majesty's bedroom. Fagan later claimed he intended to slash his wrists with the broken glass, taking his own life in front of the Queen.[4]

The fallout from the greatest breach of royal security in the twentieth century was as dramatic as one would expect. Amid much public outrage, police resignations were tendered, Scotland Yard investigated, and Prime Minister Margaret Thatcher personally apologized to Her Majesty for the danger posed by an intruder who so easily strolled through what should have been one of the most heavily guarded homes in the world. In the eye of this storm, one that easily could have ended with deadly collateral damage, the Queen proved herself to be the calm, courageous person she has always been.

The visit from Michael Fagan was not the first time Queen Elizabeth stared danger in the face as the result of her role as monarch, nor, unfortunately, would it be the last. Just a little over a year previously, a teenager had fired shots at her during the Trooping the Colour parade. Each June this annual military showcase celebrates the national holiday honoring the sovereign's birthday. Riding sidesaddle on her favorite mount, a nineteen-year-old black mare named Burmese, the Queen had passed by thousands of spectators crowding the Mall and was just turning right to lead the Household Cavalry when Marcus Sarjeant pushed through the cheering crowd, brandishing what appeared to be a handgun.

The weapon turned out to be a mail-order replica of a Colt Python that only fired blanks, but of course no one knew this until after Sarjeant was apprehended and arrested. In the moment, it appeared to be an assassination attempt on the Queen's life. As police and civilians instantly descended on Sarjeant, the Queen reined in Burmese, naturally startled and breaking canter, then patted his neck and offered a soothing word. During the entire incident, the Queen did not flinch, did not turn, and did not appear alarmed in any way. Instead, once her mount was steadied, she smiled reassuringly at the crowd as three cavalry guards on horseback closed in around her. Both the public and the press took notice, praising her "guts, courage, pluck, bravery and bottle."[5]

Prince Charles, who was riding behind his mother with his father, Prince Philip, watched the incident again for a BBC documentary celebrating the Queen's ninetieth birthday in 2016, commenting, "She is a marvelous rider. She has a marvelous way with horses. . . . She's made of strong stuff, you know."[6] The future king seemed reticent to acknowledge the potential threat on his mother's life, keeping the focus on her equestrian skills and strength of character. Royal biographer Sally Bedell Smith echoes the Prince of Wales's understatement: "The Queen's reaction was not only an impressive display of expert horsemanship, but the first time the public had witnessed so vividly the unflinching physical courage and equilibrium that friends and courtiers had seen privately."[7]

Her Majesty the Queen moments before shots were fired from the crowd during Trooping the Colour, June 13, 1981.
Bob Thomas/Popperfoto/Getty Images

Apparently, Elizabeth has always been known for her fortitude, fearlessness, and unflappable grace under pressure. Whether riding her beloved horses without a helmet, which she has done since first learning to ride at age three, traveling in an open-air carriage when visiting non-Commonwealth countries, or staring down statesmen twice her age, such as Churchill, the Queen relies on her instincts as much as her intelligence. She does not take unnecessary chances and listens closely to cautions from her staff and security detail. But ultimately, Her Majesty refuses to allow fear to play a role in any of her decisions.

By this point in her reign, the Queen had already endured several would-be assassination attempts. Less than a month before teen assailant Marcus Sarjeant's scare, a bomb had blasted an oil terminal at British Petroleum's new refinery in Scotland during Queen Elizabeth's opening remarks just five hundred yards away. The Irish Republican Army (IRA) claimed responsibility.[8] The terrorist organization had long been at war against the monarchy, the symbol of the British Commonwealth, which they held responsible for dividing their nation.

Among its many fatal acts, the IRA had shocked the world by killing Lord Louis Mountbatten two years prior in 1979. A bomb had been placed aboard Mountbatten's boat, which he was known to enjoy during annual summer holidays in Ireland. The blast killed him, along with one of his young grandsons and the boy's paternal grandmother.

Known as Uncle Dickie to the Royal Family, Mountbatten was an iconic presence throughout twentieth-century British history, serving as First Sea Lord, the head of the Royal Navy, and the last Viceroy of India prior to its independence. Mountbatten, the great-grandson of Queen Victoria and second cousin to Queen Elizabeth II, influenced and mentored Prince Charles, who referred to Mountbatten as his "honorary Grandfather" and openly wept at the death of the seventy-nine-year-old World War II naval hero.[9] In 2018 the third child of William and Catherine, the Duke and Duchess of Cambridge, was named in honor of Lord Mountbatten.

The IRA bombing issued a wake-up call of sorts. After such an egregious act of violent terrorism, security measures were supposedly tightened on the Royal Family, but as revealed by the incidents in Scotland, at the Trooping of the Colour, and in Buckingham Palace, obviously not tightened enough. And apparently, not all attempts to harm the Queen during that time were made public. In 2018 secret documents were declassified that revealed that Christopher John Lewis, another seventeen-year-old would-be shooter, had fired a .22 rifle at Queen Elizabeth during a royal visit to New Zealand in 1981.

As Her Majesty and Prince Philip rode in a parade in the city of Dunedin, Lewis perched on the fifth floor of a nearby building. He had planned and prepared to assassinate the visiting monarch, later claiming he commanded a terrorist cell called the National Imperial Guerilla Army, which he eventually acknowledged as fictional. When onlookers reported hearing a gunshot fired in the vicinity of the Queen, local police assured them it was merely a large sign falling over amid the jostling crowd.

This denial proved to be one of the dangling threads of the blanket cover-up by the New Zealand Security Intelligence Service, which finally released details of Lewis's assassination plot. When their secret documents were declassified, reports revealed that "Lewis did indeed originally intend to assassinate the Queen but did not have a suitable vantage point from which to fire, nor a sufficiently high-powered rifle for the range."[10] The cover-up apparently resulted from the fears of leaders at the time, who worried that knowledge of the incident might prevent future royal visits.

While investigative reporters and conspiracy theorists proved vindicated by the disclosure, it's unclear when, or even if, the Queen or her security team had been informed of Lewis's attempt. In keeping with Her Majesty's response to so many dangerous situations and sensational plots, the palace had no comment.

How many more such attempts have been kept under wraps or have gone undiscovered? While only a handful of incidents are included here, it seems likely that there were probably many more, known and unknown. Perhaps this is to be expected because of the high profile of her iconic role, similar to the kind of dangerous attention attracted by US presidents, Catholic popes, or international celebrities. Given that, what's conspicuous about the incidents Queen Elizabeth has faced is their blessedly benign outcome. Her courage and composure serve her well, but one also wonders whether there is a measure of divine protection.

Perhaps the royal anthem of "God Save the Queen" is inherently a prayer.

Queen Elizabeth would later tell family and friends that she couldn't believe her eyes when she saw Sarjeant firing his weapon at almost point-blank range. Still, she maintained the calm poise of a courageous leader confident in her fate. Those close to her have long observed that the Queen seems rather fatalistic about the possibility of assassination, refusing to limit her visibility and interactions with the subjects she serves. Perhaps rather than fatalistic, Queen Elizabeth trusts that the God who chose her to lead her nation would also protect her according to his almighty sovereignty and divine providence.

She refuses to give in to the fear that would be quite natural and justifiable given her role and high profile. Instead, she calls to mind the faithful courage and courageous faith shown by God's people throughout the pages of the Bible and the annals of history. Her steely resolve calls to mind the fearlessness of King David facing Goliath, the resourcefulness of Queen Esther saving her people, and the faithfulness of the prophet Daniel thrust into the Babylonian lions' den.

In her ability to remain unshaken in the face of danger, Queen Elizabeth II carries on a proud legacy of royal leadership worthy of any of her predecessors. In her we see hints of the indomitable spirit of King Henry V, who won the Battle of Agincourt in 1415 against the French and united the English people. We glimpse the shrewd diplomacy of her namesake, Queen Elizabeth I, who used her gender as an asset amid the cultural limitations of her day. And we witness the faithful heart of Queen Victoria, her great-great-grandmother, who managed to combine the majestic with the domestic in serving her subjects with dedicated devotion.

Queen Elizabeth II watched her parents endure the abdication crisis and World War II, surviving these tests through sheer determination and steadfast faith. Her father embraced a role he never wanted or expected and led Britain through the darkest days of the twentieth century. Her mother became a common-sense crusader for doing what was right even when it required self-sacrifice. She made sure her daughter recognized that only faith could sustain her through all the trials, both personal and public, that she would inevitably encounter as the reigning monarch of an empire in transition.

Consequently, Queen Elizabeth has demonstrated time and time again a steely determination to lead without flinching. Sir Edward Ford, the Queen's assistant private secretary for a decade and a half, once said, "I never saw her scared in any way," noting that even when Irish protestors once lobbed a large rock at her car during a visit to Belfast, Her Majesty didn't flinch but drove on as if nothing had happened."[11]

Such mettle transcends human capacity. Quite simply, Queen Elizabeth II remains calm in any crisis because she has placed her trust in God. It's not only part of her temperament but also obedience to her King: "Have I not commanded you? Be strong and courageous. Do not be afraid; do not be discouraged, for the LORD your God will be with you wherever you go" (Joshua 1:9).

Staring down would-be assailants and calming rambunctious horses aren't the only times the Queen has exercised her considerable courage. Despite the conservative nature of her role and the historically reserved British culture, Her Majesty knows when to risk for the right reasons. In one of her greatest political coups, Queen Elizabeth diverted Soviet influence in the Commonwealth country of Ghana as it struggled for independence.

By 1961 Her Majesty was nearing completion of her first decade as ruling monarch of Britain and the Commonwealth. John F. Kennedy had been inaugurated as the youngest elected president in US history, and Soviet Premier Nikita Khrushchev was building a wall to separate East and West Berlin. Into this mix, other world leaders danced around the waltz of these superpowers, including Kwame Nkrumah, the ruler of a former Commonwealth member, the nation of Ghana.

As global tensions heated up with the Cold War, many of the newly independent, developing nations in Africa, including Ghana, became diplomatic chessboards for political games. These matches pitted the Soviets against leaders from the US and her allies, including Britain. With a wealth of untapped natural resources to offer, these African nations often sought recognition and respect through militarization and the installation of Western weaponry. Nkrumah, a smart and savvy leader who had been educated in the US and Britain, intended to use Cold War tensions to advance his own socialist agendas.

Nkrumah had escaped imprisonment after an anticolonial strike for independence turned violent. Running for head of his party from his cell, Nkrumah not only won the election but secured his freedom as an active member of Parliament. From there he became Africa's most powerful leader, orchestrating Ghana's transition from Commonwealth member to independent nation. In the process, he learned how to use the media, particularly newspapers, to his advantage, frequently staging photo opportunities depicting him as a larger-than-life personality.

Nkrumah was determined to shake off colonial influence from its mother country and implement what he called "African socialism." To fulfill the goal of more rapid modernization, the charismatic leader had made no secret of his conversations with the Soviets. Although still a voluntary member of the Commonwealth, Ghana was clearly in transition and likely to break British ties completely.

When Prime Minister Harold Macmillan informed

Queen Elizabeth of the civil unrest and Soviet influence in Ghana, Her Majesty determined to take matter into her own hands and make an immediate trip to visit Nkrumah in his capital. The catalyst for her decision is unknown, but in one of the best-known episodes of *The Crown*, "Dear Mrs. Kennedy," creator-producer-writer Peter Morgan speculates that a snide remark by First Lady Jackie Kennedy may have been the spark.

As Morgan imagines it, Mrs. Kennedy, after a state dinner with her husband at Buckingham Palace, slights the Queen as being "incurious, unintelligent, and unremarkable."[12] The biting remark makes its way back to Her Majesty, who already felt intimidated and insecure in the shadow of the glamorous popularity enjoyed by the beautiful First Lady, at least as depicted in this episode. Learning of the simmering crisis in Ghana, the Queen seizes an opportunity to visit and handle the matter herself rather than send Macmillan or other British diplomats.

Her meeting with Nkrumah, both in life and in the episode, culminated with the two dancing the foxtrot together at the invitation of the Queen. The offer was a surprisingly bold move for a monarch known for staying out of both national and international affairs. But the Queen knew Nkrumah would not miss a photo op with the most powerful woman in the world. Whether or not this dance altered Ghana's relationship with the Soviet Union remains debatable. It did, however, close the growing distance between the African nation and its former parent.

Regardless, the dance showed Queen Elizabeth's willingness to break with tradition, ignore her advisors' cautions, and prove her strength as an individual, a monarch, and a world leader. Nkrumah could have refused her offer—he himself felt self-conscious about his dancing skills—or the two could have danced and stepped on each other's toes, literally and figuratively. Instead, the pair glided across the dance floor, demonstrating the unexpected benefit of taking a risk—grit and grace in tandem.

Queen Elizabeth dances with Ghanaian President Kwame Nkrumah, November 20, 1961.
Central Press/Getty Images

Regardless of what most British subjects think of the monarchy and Queen Elizabeth, they unanimously respect her fearless strength of character. Such admiration emerged in a conversation I had with a former palace communications staff member. With straight blond hair and a celebrity-wattage smile, she rose from the café table where she had been seated, shook my hand, and greeted me warmly.

Referred to me by two friends of friends, Bridget, as I'll call her, had worked at Buckingham Palace shortly after completing university in 2001. "I can't believe that's been nearly twenty years ago! The time—where did it go? I'm an old woman myself now, aren't I? No, don't answer that, lad!" Dressed conservatively in a dove-gray dress and an embroidered cardigan, Bridget looked posh and professional. But her vivacious, bubbly personality made it easy to see how she quickly created connections with everyone around her.

Revealing that she was not from an aristocratic or wealthy family, Bridget shared how she had parlayed her intelligence and comedic charm into a professional career in communications and public relations. "My time at the palace was more like a paid internship, really," she explained. "A lucky break for a girl from the Midlands." From there she was hired away by a firm specializing in sensitive issues and crisis management. There she met the man who became her husband. After taking a break to have their two children, she worked from home part-time and enjoyed the freedom and flexibility so much that she created her own small PR firm. Her husband had recently quit his corporate position to work with her full-time.

"The palace was a fascinating place. Surreal, really. Historical but also timeless. I was only there a year or so," she said, "and I'm sure I signed all the nondisclosure docs that were part of my packet. But I don't believe I'm violating them if I tell you that I thoroughly enjoyed my encounters with Her

Majesty, brief as they were." Like most all of the individuals in the Queen's orbit, Bridget refused to go on the record with our conversation about her time at Buckingham Palace.

In my experience trying to speak with former staff and primary acquaintances of Queen Elizabeth, I received the most polite responses, "declining the opportunity but wishing me well in my endeavour," as one leader in the Church of England had replied. They all know how much the Queen hates disclosures about both personal and professional encounters with her.

The reasons are obvious, particularly in our culture of ubiquitous social media updates. The shift in media coverage in the eighties and nineties to no-holds-barred salacious scandal and sensational intrusion, of course, is largely to blame. All the disclosures about the affairs and infidelities in her children's marriages, many with intimate details obtained unethically, if not illegally, forced the palace to realize how much control they had lost—virtually all of it—since the days when a discreet call from a palace office could squelch a front-page revelation.

Going back to 1849, Queen Victoria's husband and royal consort, Prince Albert, won a precedent-setting court decision when he sued publisher William Strange for trying to profit from *Sketches of Her Majesty's Household*, a small book featuring private etchings Albert had made of family members and favorite dogs. The case established the beginning of confidence law in England and outlined the boundary between royal privacy and public curiosity for over a century.

Among a dozen or so breaches of trust from staff members, including the betrayal of Marion Crawford, the governess known as "Crawfie" who played a large role in the childhoods of Elizabeth and Margaret Rose, left a lingering scar. Crawford's disclosures about the royal household in a memoir as well as a syndicated advice column seem relatively harmless by today's standards but felt invasive and exploitive to a family accustomed to maintaining privacy, and mystique, behind palace walls.

In 1983 Queen Elizabeth II had reached her limit with such revelatory breaches of confidence by staff when she made the unprecedented move of suing *The Sun*, a Rupert Murdoch–owned tabloid with the largest circulation in Britain at the time. A former kitchen staff, Kieran Kenny, had sold embellished accounts of life at Buckingham Palace primarily focused on then-single Prince Andrew's involvement with American soft-porn actress Koo Stark. Seeing the paper use the lawsuit to generate publicity, the Queen quickly accepted an out-of-court settlement negotiated by her attorneys. Since then, the palace has tangled legally with *The Sun* a number of times, preventing disclosure of not only confidential material but also entirely fabricated information.

No wonder, then, that so many individuals wished to remain silent or anonymous in their comments to me, even when they were unreservedly positive, as most of them were. Since the people were accustomed to an invasive class of journalists willing to do anything for a story, many of my queries were met with suspicious responses, despite my emphasis on writing an inspiring exploration of Her Majesty's faith. That I wanted to spotlight the Queen's personal faith and not necessarily her institutional roles in the Church of England was met with even greater skepticism. Even as church attendance has dwindled and the number of self-identified Christians has plummeted, most Brits would not consider it polite or appropriate to discuss religious beliefs so publicly.

Nonetheless, my limited number of interviews and spontaneous conversations proved insightful. My conversation with Bridget was no exception.

"Oh, I probably could be on record," she mused. "It might even help business a bit, I suppose. But I've learned to play it safe and not to mention anything, even innocuous as it might be, that might come back to bite me. Strange times we live in, you know?"

I confirmed that I did know, indeed, and we briefly sidetracked to discuss the present political turmoil in the US. "I'm sorry, but your lot in Washington is better than anything on telly! Who needs *Spooks* or—what's your show with the beautiful young woman shagging the president? Yes, that's it—*Scandal*! Who needs those when you've got something infinitely more entertaining!"

When asked whether she helped manage any delicate PR issues during her time at the palace, Bridget hesitated before saying, "Wouldn't you like to know?" with a teasing smile. "No, it was rather boring, actually. This would be early aughts, and the most sensitive issue involved Camilla, now the Duchess of Cornwall. She and Prince Charles were not engaged yet but clearly on their way to the altar. He wanted his mother's blessing, of course, as well as public acceptance. But that was going to take time . . . after Princess Diana, well, you know?" Bridget raised an eyebrow before sipping her spritzer.

"How were your interactions with Her Majesty the Queen?" I asked.

Nodding, Bridget said, "Fabulous! Strictly business but gracious, professional, and keen on treating you like a human being. She's brilliant, really. No one—and I mean *no one*—can do what she does. The Queen inspired me to push myself. I've never really said that before, but it's true. Her strength has depth, you know?"

I nodded and smiled at her unbridled admiration. "What about her faith? What role does it play in her strength?"

She thought for a moment before shrugging. "Honestly, I couldn't say. But I know she must have faith. You don't endure and thrive unless there's more inside your heart. She's fearless, she is!" Bridget continued.

"What did you think of her participation in the opening of the Olympic Games in 2012?" I asked. "That bit with Daniel Craig as Bond."

"*Brilliant*! Unequivocally brilliant!" she gushed, her voice rising. "Who does *that*? I actually know someone who was on that shoot—unbelievable! And it was so fitting. She's every bit as tough as James Bond."

In yet another unprecedented surprise, the Queen had filmed a brief segment in which the actor, in character as his superspy screen persona, visits Buckingham Palace and escorts Her Majesty, with a parcel of corgis trailing behind them down the hall, to board a waiting helicopter outside. As the giant screen in London's Olympic Stadium faded to black, the whirring copter settled overhead as its two iconic passengers parachuted to the arena floor below. Coming off the field, the Queen—dressed identically to her stunt double—smiled and waved before taking her seat in the royal box.

"She's absolutely larger than life, our Liz! She's what

you'd get if your granny became one of the Avengers." She punctuated her comparison with a giggle, which made me now feel more like an old friend rather than a new acquaintance.

"To Her Majesty," I said, raising my glass. "Cheers!"

"Cheers, luv," Bridget said, lifting her glass as well. "To Her Majesty! God save the Queen!"

For me, the life of Jesus Christ, the Prince of Peace . . . is an inspiration and an anchor in my life. A role model of reconciliation and forgiveness, he stretched out his hands in love, acceptance and healing. Christ's example has taught me to seek to respect and value all people, of whatever faith or none.

—annual Christmas broadcast, 2014

chapter seven

EXAMPLE *and* EXEMPLAR

TREATING OTHERS AS YOU
WISH TO BE TREATED

*T*hrowing a party after a major home renovation might not seem so unusual. After all, most homeowners would want to celebrate repairs and improvements, particularly ones requiring five years and millions of dollars. Inviting over a thousand contractors, carpenters, and craftworkers as the guests of honor, however, could be done only by Her Majesty Queen Elizabeth II.

Almost five years to the day after a spotlight ignited a curtain and started a major fire at Windsor Castle, Queen Elizabeth hosted a party there to celebrate its complete restoration. It had been nearly three months since the death of Princess Diana, and the Royal Family had begun taking steps back toward their usual schedules and regular routines. Returning to London in November, Her Majesty celebrated two enormous milestones: the restoration of her favorite residence and her fiftieth wedding anniversary.

Prince Philip had supervised the restoration of Windsor, along with help from son Prince Charles, himself an expert enthusiast on historical architecture and art. Located about thirty miles west of London and situated on the Thames River, Windsor occupies thirteen acres of gardens and gateways, terraces and towers, courtyards and cloisters. The castle was originally built by William the Conqueror in the eleventh century after his successful Norman conquest of England. King Henry I, William's fourth son, established royal residency at Windsor in the early twelfth century, making it the largest and longest-occupied castle in Europe.

Windsor's campus is comprised of three wards based on ascending elevation: lower, middle, and upper. The fire destroyed or damaged over a hundred rooms in the upper part, necessitating its closure to the public. But the two lower wards remained open to visitors. In fact, 70 percent of the $61 million repair cost was funded by entrance fees for tours of the castle as well as those generated by tours of Buckingham Palace, which opened its doors to summer tourists for the first time, expressly to raise restoration funds for Windsor. The other 30 percent came from government money annually budgeted for upkeep of the royal residences. The director of media affairs for the Royal Collection Trust at the time, Dickie Arbiter, stressed, "This has been done at no extra cost to the taxpayer."[1] The restoration also came in under budget by almost $5 million, with work completed six months ahead of schedule.

Notably, in repairing and refurbishing Windsor, the Queen agreed with the suggestion of her husband and oldest son to restore and enhance the essence of its grandeur rather than undertake a painstaking recreation of what it had been. This decision resulted in significant changes to St. George's

Hall and the Private Chapel, rendering a modern reinterpretation of the castle's distinct Gothic and Georgian aesthetic.

Windsor Castle, circa 1900.
Archive Photos/Stringer/Getty Images

The finished spaces included details both old and new. A Gothic hammer beam with crisscrossing arches and struts made of green oak replaced the painted plaster ceiling in the great banqueting hall of Saint George. In the chapel, stained glass window panels depict a firefighter aiming a hose at a burning tower, while another shows a hard-hatted worker moving a painting to safety. These images were inspired by sketches and notes Prince Philip made shortly after the fire.

As with so many other facets of the monarchy, Queen Elizabeth and the Royal Family managed to modernize something ancient while retaining its essence, making it even better than before.

During the grand reopening gala hosted by the Queen to honor those responsible for Windsor's dramatic restoration, one incident stands out. Her Majesty and the Duke of Edinburgh made a point of thanking each of the more than 1,500 guests in attendance for their contribution to the magnificent result. One carpenter of Pakistani descent was particularly thrilled to meet the Queen, and after their brief exchange, later returned to her side. "Your Majesty, Your Majesty, please come with me. I want you to meet someone," he exclaimed.

Without missing a beat, the Queen smiled as the carpenter led her across the room and introduced her to his brother. The workman thanked her profusely, and she returned to mingling with other guests. A few minutes later, however, the same carpenter returned and once again requested that Her Majesty accompany him to meet another brother, who had actually assisted in carving some of the castle's restored woodwork. Once again, the Queen graciously accompanied the man and thanked his brother for his fine work.

Rather than mind the interruption—not once but *twice*—Queen Elizabeth served her guest with kindness rather than take offense at his severe breach of both etiquette and royal protocol. Allegedly, Her Majesty enjoyed the incident so much that she often shared the anecdote with friends and visiting dignitaries, ending with the punch line: "I began to worry that he might have twelve brothers!"[2]

Queen Elizabeth's gracious interaction with the excited carpenter exemplifies the way she deals with virtually everyone she encounters. Simply put, she follows the Golden Rule of treating others the way she wants to be treated. While some critics of the monarchy consider her public interactions as pandering to populism, most people who actually meet Her Majesty know that she is not contriving her interest in their lives. One only has to consider the way politicians typically glad-hand and feign interest in prospective voters to know the difference.

From staff who interact with her daily to veterans receiving commendations, from community leaders to Olympic athletes, and from schoolchildren to small business owners, the Queen finds a way to connect with them. She's good at engaging in the present moment and finding a common interest, a shared experience, or an obvious reference point, such as the weather, sports, or history.

When meeting event organizers and on-site hosts, Queen Elizabeth often apologizes for causing traffic delays or upsetting normal routines. She's incredibly punctual and expects the same of those around her. Nonetheless, she's been known to linger when meeting with victims of tragedies or guests with whom she shares a personal connection. She doesn't correct those who stray from royal protocol and seems not to mind if someone, like the carpenter at Windsor, becomes overly enthusiastic.

The Queen often uses humor to bond with others and loves to share stories, often mimicking the voices of those involved. She's not easily embarrassed or offended, as many nervous individuals have discovered. Photographer Harry Benson once met Her Majesty to do a shoot at Buckingham Palace. Nervous about what to say during their time together, he commented on the Queen's beloved corgis dozing nearby, eventually asking her whether she slept with them. "No, because they snore," she responded.[3]

While other family members, particularly Princess Margaret and the Queen Mother, seemed at times to revel in royal privilege, Queen Elizabeth rarely if ever makes a fuss. She doesn't mind cooking a meal, cleaning up after herself, or tromping through muddy stables. Even as a girl, when given an opportunity she enjoyed mingling with other children from backgrounds less privileged than her own.

She actively participated in the Girl Guides, the British version of Girl Scouts, while staying at Windsor during World War II, warmly welcoming new members who joined the troop after their families were forced to leave London during the Blitz. These tough city girls with Cockney accents called her Lilibet, while well-bred daughters of aristocracy knew to avoid such familiarity with the King's daughter. The city girls assumed their pal Lilibet wanted to learn to bake scones and wash dishes afterward as much as they did, unaware of the staff who served the future queen on a daily basis.

When she was eighteen, Princess Elizabeth enjoyed a similar experience when she joined the Auxiliary Territorial Service (ATS), the women's branch of the British Army during World War II. Despite her parents' reluctance, she persisted in her determination to serve alongside other young adult women and soon enlisted as Second Subaltern Elizabeth Alexandra Mary Windsor.

While the rank was honorary, her training was just as hands-on and comprehensive as that of the other female recruits. "The Princess is to be treated in exactly the same way as any other officer learning at the driving training centre," the official report stated. Elizabeth did her part and seemed to enjoy such mundane chores as serving in the mess hall and learning the basics of engine maintenance.

In six weeks she had qualified as a lorry driver and been promoted to junior commander. The war ended soon after and halted her budding military career, but the memorable experience lingered. Decades later Queen Elizabeth told Barbara Castle, an influential Labour Party politician, that her stint with the ATS was the only time in her life when she had been able to compare her own capabilities to those of her peers.[4]

This comment likely reveals more than the Queen intended about the lonely, often isolated nature of her position. Which also explains why she enjoys meeting ordinary people so much, revealing her curiosity about who they are and how they see the world, whether they're a horse trainer or a head of state. She's naturally a student of human nature and delights in recognizing the shared similarities among diverse people rather than allowing differences to separate them.

While the Queen certainly enjoys meeting and interacting with her subjects, those encounters are likely easier than the many situations in which she's forced to engage as head of state. Her role as reigning monarch requires that she regularly interact with domestic politicians, particularly the prime minister, as well as international dignitaries, officials, and leaders. Naturally, some of these relationships are more challenging than others, especially considering the more than six decades Her Majesty has reigned.

She is far too gracious and discreet to speak critically about anyone, but one suspects that some personalities have grated more than others. Many political pundits and royal observers believe it likely that one of the most challenging was someone who, having much in common with the Queen, should have been a confidant. After all, she and Margaret Thatcher were only about six months apart in age. Nonetheless, their different backgrounds, and more likely their distinct personalities and dispositions, kept their relationship strictly professional.

Although their social status differed, their ascent to power ran parallel in many ways. Shortly after Queen Elizabeth's coronation, a young Thatcher, then an up-and-coming Conservative politician, wrote a newspaper column praising the new queen's opportunity to "remove the last shreds of prejudice against women aspiring to the highest places" so that "a new era for women will indeed be at hand."[5] A quarter-century later, Thatcher reached that highest place, leading her party in a sweeping victory to become the first female prime minister in British history.

Thatcher would also become the longest-serving PM of the twentieth century, leading the nation through a tumultuous economic recession, the Falklands War, and dramatic world events, including the fall of the Berlin Wall and the end of apartheid in South Africa. Thatcher's tenure began on the heels of a period of national strife in 1978–79 known as the Winter of Discontent. The brutally cold, snowy season featured widespread strikes by trade unions in public sector jobs, including truck drivers, garbage collectors, and maintenance workers.

Thatcher implemented a series of social and economic policies, collectively known as Thatcherism, to remediate and reverse the soaring unemployment rate and hard economic times across Britain. Her political philosophy and economic agenda reflected many of the beliefs held by her greatest non-British ally, US President Ronald Reagan, whose two terms overlapped with the center of Thatcher's tenure. Like Reagan, Thatcher promoted deregulation of business, privatization of government-owned companies, and a large, flexible labor pool detached from the unifying power and political influence of labor unions.

She cut the personal income tax rate and nearly doubled the value-added tax (VAT), increased interest rates to slow and control the public money supply, and dramatically reduced government spending on social services such as education and housing. At first, Thatcher's policies seemed to be working but quickly resulted in an economic backlash that deepened the recession and resulted in public riots during the early eighties.

Dubbed the "Iron Lady" because of her firm, no-nonsense commitment to her policies and political convictions, Thatcher took a particularly hard line against trade and labor unions, believing they harmed the general public as well as the average workers whose best interests they claimed to represent. Thatcher introduced numerous pieces of legislation to limit the power of unions, and while the largest ones fought back through strikes and lobbying, they lost ground.

Thatcher's opposition to unions moved front and center in a defining and devastating battle with the National Union of Mineworkers (NUM). When the National Coal Board announced plans to close twenty of the 174 state-owned mines, roughly two-thirds of Britain's coal miners went on strike. The national strike was declared illegal by the High Court of Justice, and Thatcher refused to meet any of NUM's demands, labeling their leaders as "the enemy within" and comparing their resistance to Argentina's attempt to reclaim the Falklands from the Commonwealth.

Images of police and military presence trying to contain angry protesters with riot gear became regular front-page fare for most newspapers and tabloids. The British working class felt attacked, punished by a government that seemed authoritarian and unsympathetic as it enforced Thatcher's policies. While Queen Elizabeth made no public comment on the divisive impasse, she undoubtedly worried about the detrimental impact on her subjects.

The strike lasted for a full year before NUM's leadership ended it in March 1985 without achieving any of its demands. The strike's economic blow was estimated at roughly £1.5 billion, resulting in a dramatic fall against the US dollar. By 1986 the British government under Thatcher had closed twenty-five unprofitable coal mines, and by the time she resigned in 1990, the number had climbed toward one hundred, many of which had remained profitable. The rest were privatized. As a result, tens of thousands of jobs were lost, reducing entire communities to ghost towns.

It wasn't only Margaret Thatcher's domestic policies that Queen Elizabeth likely struggled to support. In her cost-cutting pragmatism, the prime minister took aim at the Commonwealth nations' relationship to their mother country. For example, Thatcher implemented higher tuition fees for international students from Commonwealth nations; they had previously enjoyed the same rates as British nationals attending university in the United Kingdom. Trade regulations and tariffs between members of the Commonwealth and the UK were similarly scrutinized and tightened when possible.

Perhaps of even more concern to the Queen was Thatcher's attitude toward social and cultural struggles over apartheid within the Commonwealth nations of Rhodesia and South Africa. When Thatcher assumed office, she faced considerable international pressure to implement British sanctions against these two nations, but she feared the economic impact on Britain's international businesses. She also refused to endorse initiatives for equality made by black nationals in the Commonwealth's African nations. Thatcher wasn't unsympathetic to their cause but remained singularly focused on domestic issues, considering the vast reach of the Commonwealth a drain on energy, attention, and resources.

Two incidents in particular show the way Queen Elizabeth handled the tension over these matters with her prime minister. The first involved the meeting held every two years to bring the leaders of all Commonwealth governments together to discuss shared initiatives and to set common goals. The meeting was scheduled to be in Lusaka, Zambia, the year Thatcher became PM, and the Queen, who had missed only one of these summits in almost three decades, intended to attend. Her Majesty considered it especially important to meet with the leaders of the African Commonwealth nations and to show her concern for their struggles toward independence and racial equality.

Right before the meeting was to take place that summer, Rhodesian security forces bombed nearby Lusaka, targeting guerilla insurgents. The city was called a war zone by other Commonwealth leaders who were increasingly nervous about the Queen's presence in such a volatile, potentially violent environment. Thatcher expressly tried to prevent her sovereign from attending because of the risk involved. Undeterred, Queen Elizabeth embarked on a nine-day, four-nation tour of African Commonwealth nations prior to her arrival in Lusaka two days ahead of her prime minister.

There, in her role as Head of the Commonwealth, the Queen hosted a reception and banquet for all forty-two leaders, remaining until midnight to ensure that she spoke with each one. Throughout the next few days, Her Majesty also worked behind the scenes to reduce tensions and increase unity within the Commonwealth by hosting each national leader for a private visit in her bungalow. Each chat lasted around twenty minutes as the Queen asked specific questions unique to each leader's country and government and offered her support and understanding of the challenges they faced.

She particularly expressed her support for the African Commonwealth leaders, demonstrating a remarkable depth of understanding of the complex variables intertwined in each nation's struggle for racial equality. They were impressed not only with her knowledge but also her willingness to engage and to care about their respective needs as a nation. While she never directed their actions or gave advice, she once again served as the guiding force—the royal glue as it were—holding such a large, disparate group of Commonwealth nations together. "I am convinced that the intervention spurred the organization—which was on the point of possibly splitting up—on to compromise," Chief Emeka Anyaoku of Nigeria later recalled.[6]

Before the summit's end, the Queen's intervention paved the way for Thatcher to sign the Lusaka Accord, a multinational agreement calling for a constitutional conference to be convened later that year in London. Sure enough, by December 1984, the London convocation yielded an agreement calling for a cease-fire, free elections, and national independence for Rhodesia, which would thereafter be known as the Republic of Zimbabwe. The Commonwealth's secretary-general at the time, Sonny Ramphal of Guyana, later looked back at the Queen's role and observed, "The fact that she was there made it happen."[7]

Despite the relative success of such an auspicious collaborative effort at the beginning of the PM's tenure, initiated largely by the Queen, the relationship between Her Majesty and Mrs. Thatcher deteriorated over the next few years. While there are many reasons, one of the largest involved Thatcher's response to another Commonwealth nation in crisis. Even as international pressure, both within and beyond the Commonwealth, mounted on South Africa to end apartheid, Thatcher refused to impose economic and trade sanctions. This tactic was employed by a number of other world leaders, including the United States, which passed the Comprehensive Anti-Apartheid Act of 1986, a law listing specific sanctions against South Africa and the conditions for removing them.

Thatcher insisted that imposing sanctions would damage British exports while also harming the South African citizens they were intended to help. Many leaders agreed that sanctions would hurt the working-class, mostly black, population in the short term but deemed sanctions necessary to precipitate any long-term government change abolishing apartheid. By 1986 Thatcher had also learned to play a more sophisticated political game, delivering bold declarations and passionate rhetoric at conferences with other leaders while delaying any implied follow-up action.

Then everything came to a head. On July 20, 1986, the morning edition of *The Sunday Times* ran a shocking front-page headline: "Queen dismayed by 'uncaring' Thatcher." Using the issue of South African sanctions as a starting point, the article alleged that, according to reliable palace sources, Queen Elizabeth found the prime minister's attitude toward many political and social issues directly affecting human lives to be "uncaring, confrontational and socially divisive."[8] The article claimed to offer unprecedented insight into the monarch's views of her nation's government leader, something the Queen had never revealed publicly in her then thirty-three-year reign.

Known for maintaining her neutrality above and beyond specific policies and people, Queen Elizabeth was outraged at such a claim, which likely contained some kernels of truth of her private feelings toward Mrs. Thatcher and her policies. She called and apologized to the prime minister immediately —by some accounts even the night before the story broke in the paper. Years later, the Queen's sister, Princess Margaret, reportedly told one of her closest friends, who revealed it in a documentary, that she saw Her Majesty cry only one time—in the wake of this article and the hurt it caused Mrs. Thatcher.[9]

The Queen's response is similarly depicted in Peter Morgan's award-winning stage play *The Audience*, which time-travels through Queen Elizabeth's weekly meetings with a dozen prime ministers over sixty years. In the scene showing Thatcher's meeting with the Queen the week after the *Sunday Times* article, Her Majesty, portrayed once again by Helen Mirren, literally shakes in dread right before Thatcher enters. Thatcher unleashes her hurt and fury at the Queen, who quietly takes it before trying to change the topic to "the business at hand," at which Thatcher roars, "This *is* the business at hand!"[10]

The journalist responsible for the article maintained the credibility of his palace sources, which was quickly revealed to be only one person, Michael Shea, the Queen's press secretary. Shea had willingly given the interview but claimed his words had been taken out of context and erroneously attributed to Her Majesty. Nonetheless, the damage was done. Mrs. Thatcher made no public response and refused to acknowledge the incident, even later in her memoirs.

Despite whatever differences they may have had, the Queen wasted no time in apologizing to Mrs. Thatcher and seemed to hold a softer view of her prime minister for the remaining few years of her service. Shortly after Thatcher resigned in 1990, choosing to withdraw from a vote within her own party challenging her leadership, Queen Elizabeth awarded Thatcher two of the Crown's most prestigious honors, the Order of the Garter and the Order of Merit. Each order never has more than twenty-four members at a time, making membership quite exclusive and reserved for individuals who have proved themselves worthy through considerable contributions over time.

The Queen had bestowed the Order of the Garter on only three previous PMs, most notably Winston Churchill, but the Order of Merit was usually awarded to academics, scientists, and historians. Reading between the lines, perhaps, it seems that Her Majesty rewarded Thatcher both for her almost-twelve years of service as Prime Minister as well as for her studious, ever-curious, methodical intellect. The dual awards also reflected Mrs. Thatcher's career pursuits. She had studied chemistry in college and worked as a research chemist before pursuing law and becoming a barrister, which launched her political career.

Mrs. Thatcher continued to serve as a member of Parliament in the House of Commons until retiring in 1992. She then received the honor of a life peerage from the Queen, entitling her as Baroness Thatcher to sit in the House of Lords. After her husband's death from cancer in 2003, Baroness Thatcher began to suffer from dementia, which would compound other health problems until her death from a stroke in 2013 at age eighty-seven. Queen Elizabeth attended the funeral, which was only the second time she had attended a former prime minister's funeral.

From overzealous carpenters to iron-willed politicians, the Queen tries to treat others as she herself wants to be treated. She enjoys interacting with regular people because she's committed to leading her subjects by serving them. She dutifully relates to other leaders with respect, courtesy, and compassion. She follows the example Christ set by remaining humble, gracious, and kind toward everyone she encounters. Despite the vast number of dignitaries and celebrities she meets, Her Majesty has always championed ordinary citizens and praised their contributions to improve the lives of others.

In her 1980 Christmas address, she said, "As I go about the country and abroad I meet many people who, all in their own ways, are making a real contribution to their community.

I come across examples of unselfish service in all walks of life and in many unexpected places."[11] Thanking viewers for their various acts of kindness and service, the Queen ended her broadcast by quoting Tennyson's poem "Ring Out, Wild Bells," overtly returning attention to Jesus's example:

> Ring in the valiant man, and free,
>> The larger heart, the kindlier hand;
>> Ring out the darkness of the land,
> Ring in the Christ that is to be.[12]

It was an unseasonably mild day in late fall, and I had taken the train from London's Paddington Station to Windsor & Eton Riverside Station. In less than an hour, the hectic bustle of the city melted into the more relaxed pace of the Berkshire countryside, home to Windsor Castle and Eton College. By the time we pulled into the station, the sun was playing hide-and-seek among a swirling handful of puffy gray clouds. The air smelled fresh and felt moist, almost springlike, not cold and damp per usual this time of year. Instead of my old Barbour jacket, which quickly became hot and cumbersome, I wore a nylon windcheater, an impulse splurge at John Lewis the day before.

After realizing I had just missed the Changing of the Guard at the castle, I bought a coffee and chocolate biscuit at the train station. I meandered outside to enjoy my snack and noticed a couple taking numerous selfies. They were striking in appearance, both with olive skin and dark hair, so attractive they could be models for a travel brochure showcasing the young, multiethnic diversity of twenty-first-century Britain.

"Would you like me to take your picture?" I offered.

"*Would* you?" the young woman said, smiling back at me. "We're rubbish at it!"

Her companion rolled his eyes at her and looked me over, perhaps wondering whether he could catch me if I made a mad dash with his phone. Realizing that I was probably twice his age and a good four or five stone heavier than his lean runner's body, he nodded and handed me the phone. "You know how . . . ?"

"I do," I said.

"Keep clicking then 'til we get the money shot," he said. There was no humor in his voice, so I wasn't quite sure how to interpret his instruction. For all I knew, they might be social media celebrities with millions of followers. I suddenly worried that my shots would be no different or better than their own.

After snapping a half-dozen or more, I returned the phone to the young man.

"Thank you," he said rather formally. "I'm Yamar, and this is my cousin Kim."

"Kimmy," she corrected, beaming.

I shook both their hands and introduced myself.

"Let's see how we did," Yamar said. "Nice! Well done, you." He scrolled through them again. "Look at this one," he said, tilting the phone screen toward his companion. "Or should we post this one?"

"Yeah, brilliant," Kimmy said. "Thanks again."

"You're very welcome. Your first time to visit Windsor?" I asked, enjoying our interaction. They reminded me of my

young adult children, something about their casual attitude
—a blend of fun, joy, and openness to the present moment.

"I've been here *loads* of times," he said at the same
moment Kimmy blurted, "Yeah, and I can't wait!"

"She's visiting," he explained. "From Mumbai."

"But I'm going to move here as soon as I can get sorted,"
she said. "And someday, I'm going to meet the Duke and
Duchess of Sussex. After all, Yaz knows the Queen!"

"Well, not exactly," he said. "My dad and my uncle
worked there. You know, after that fire they had here a long
time ago. They were electricians. My father said I was born
right around the time they finished. The Queen actually
thanked them in person, a big do and all. So now I have to
bring Kimmy here because she totally fangirl 'ships Harry
and Meghan!"

"Did you see their royal wedding?" she asked breathlessly
as if it had just happened earlier that morning. Then her eyes
instantly opened wide as a new thought occurred, and she
whispered, *"Were you here for their wedding?"*

"Did you not see me on telly?" I said with my best
poker face.

But I could hold it for only a few seconds before I burst
with laughter. "No, I'm afraid not," I said. "I don't think I
would've made the cut, but I'm flattered that you would
even think that a possibility."

Kimmy laughed with me, slightly embarrassed, and said,
"Well, you *do* look like someone who would be invited to a
royal wedding. Not American at all, really—not that you—or
they are—oh, I've put myself in it, haven't I?"

I laughed even harder, relieved as the two of them
joined in.

Grief is the price we pay for love.

—*condolence message read at
a service of remembrance in
New York City after 9/11*

chapter eight

COMFORT *and* COMPASSION

MOURNING LIFE'S LOSSES
BY CONSOLING OTHERS

"Well, shall I help you?"

Queen Elizabeth II aimed this gentle question at Dr. David Nott during a private luncheon one October afternoon in 2014. Dr. Nott served as a consultant surgeon at several London hospitals, including Royal Marsden, St. Mary's, and Chelsea and Westminster, all part of the National Health Service system in the United Kingdom. In addition to his London-based, rotating practice, Dr. Nott also volunteered several months each year with Médecins Sans Frontières and the International Red Cross in war zones and dangerous hot spots such as Afghanistan, Bosnia, and Syria.

Prior to his meeting with Her Majesty, Dr. Nott had recently returned from Aleppo, a key battleground city in the ongoing Syrian Civil War. There the surgeon had operated on victims—mostly children—of gunfire, improvised explosive devices, and missile launches from various opposing militants. He worked from a makeshift surgical theater hidden amid the dusty ruins of Aleppo's ravaged streets, where shattered limbs, blood loss, and internal organ damage were inescapable.

Dr. Nott returned home to London and his practice there but could not leave the emotional trauma of his experiences behind. His post-traumatic stress disorder hung over him like a shroud as he mentally and emotionally tried to reconcile the violent horrors he had witnessed with the normalcy of life back home. Looking back, he later acknowledged that he didn't even realize at the time just how deeply his experiences had scarred him until his lunch at the palace with Queen Elizabeth. As one of a small number of honored guests being recognized for their humanitarian aid that fall, Dr. Nott sat next to the Queen, which led to an awkward moment when she asked where he was from, later recounted in his memoir, *War Doctor*:

> I suppose she was expecting me to say, "From Hammersmith," or something like that, but I told her I had recently returned from Aleppo. "Oh," she said. "And what was that like?" My mind filled instantly with images of toxic dust, of crushed school desks, of bloodied and limbless children. . . . My bottom lip started to go and I wanted to burst into tears, but I held myself together.[1]

Dr. Nott didn't know what to say that would be appropriate but, of course, wanted to answer the Queen's question.

"I didn't know what to say," he explained. "It wasn't that I didn't want to speak to her—I just couldn't."[2] As it turned out, no words were needed as their eyes met and the Queen touched the doctor's hand. After a few moments had passed, Her Majesty then asked, "Well, shall I help you?" Confused by the Queen's question, he watched in amazement at what unfolded next:

> She then had a quiet word with one of the courtiers, who pointed to a silver box in front of her, which was full of biscuits. "These are for the dogs," she said, breaking one of the biscuits in two and giving me half. Together, we fed the corgis. "There," the Queen said. "That's so much better than talking, isn't it?"[3]

Dr. Nott couldn't believe how intuitively Queen Elizabeth recognized the depth of his trauma. For over twenty minutes, the two of them sat stroking Her Majesty's beloved corgis, feeding them bits of biscuit. He would later describe her as "warm and wonderful" with "unbelievable" compassion.[4]

Dr. Nott's experience is not an isolated example of the Queen's willingness to connect and comfort others in pain. Naturally compassionate and attuned to the people around her, Queen Elizabeth considers offering support and comfort an integral part of serving her subjects, both corporately and individually.

As a young princess during World War II, Elizabeth had witnessed how her parents welcomed displaced refugee families at Windsor Castle. They also met with families of soldiers who had given their lives in the war, as well as many injured and wounded veterans. These experiences were not the only times Elizabeth observed her royal predecessors offering comfort but were likely some of the most memorable.

Her Majesty the Queen's parents, King George VI and Queen Elizabeth, visit wounded soldiers at Preston, Lancashire, England, March 1945.
Tuson/Daily Mail/Shutterstock

Growing up, she also heard about how her grandfather sent handwritten letters to members of the Royal Military and to US servicemen in England to thank them for their service. King George V also added his blessing to chaplains serving during the war, becoming patron of their department and establishing them as The Royal Army Chaplains' Department.

His Majesty valued the role military chaplains played in ministering to soldiers and their families, particularly during wartime, by providing spiritual support, moral guidance, and pastoral care irrespective of religion or theological beliefs. Chaplains wore British Army uniforms but did not serve as combatants. They could lead and manage but not command units. Of the 179 British Army chaplains who died in World War I, three were awarded Victoria Cross medals. Queen Elizabeth II continues her grandfather's legacy and remains their patron.[5]

King George V also instituted November 11 as Remembrance Day in Commonwealth countries. Since its inception in 1919, this memorial holiday honors all the men and women who have given their lives in service to their nation and the Commonwealth, and it celebrates peaceful relationships with other countries worldwide. This day of remembrance has become synonymous with the red poppy, a symbol of remembrance adopted in 1921 based on the poem "In Flanders Fields" by John McCrae, a Canadian physician who served as a Lieutenant-Colonel during the Great War. Instead of focusing on the travesty of war and its devastating loss of life in his poem, McCrae assuaged his grief by describing small signs of hope, such as larks singing beyond the gunfire and red poppies blooming in the muddy, bloodstained fields of Flanders.

Following the example set by her grandfather and maintained by her father, Queen Elizabeth has led the nation and the Commonwealth in remembering, on the second Sunday in November, those who have died in world wars and other military conflicts. The focal point of the day's remembrance is a ceremony at the Cenotaph, a war memorial in central London, where the Queen and members of the Royal Family, along with political leaders, military officers, veterans, and thousands of others across the nation, observe two minutes of silence in honor of all fallen heroes. A single gunshot signals the start and end of the silence, followed by a bugle playing "The Last Post." The Queen places a wreath of poppies at the foot of the Cenotaph monument.[6] Though in recent years, Her Majesty has relinquished the honor of laying the memorial wreath to Prince Charles.

Traditionally, the Remembrance Day service then includes a short religious program and Scripture reading. Another bugle call provides an interlude to the singing of the national anthem, "God Save the Queen." The Queen departs the service followed by war veterans marching past the Cenotaph to honor those being remembered. As the veterans finish their slow processional march, a member of the Royal Family, such as the Duke of Edinburgh or Prince Charles, salutes them. Throughout the rest of the week, the Queen and Royal Family participate in other events to mark the solemn occasion, including concerts, church services, and the annual Festival of Remembrance at the Royal Albert Hall.

While Queen Elizabeth has occasionally been seen wiping away a tear at Remembrance Day services, royal protocol and historical precedent, not to mention her own reserved personality, typically limit the Queen's public displays of grief. Nonetheless, she is well known for offering consolation to those in mourning with whom she meets privately, such as Dr. Nott and countless others.

This dichotomy only serves to underscore the irony of the British public's demand for Her Majesty to express her mourning over the death of Princess Diana as openly as they did. In the wake of the tragic, early death of the popular People's Princess, her millions of devoted fans suddenly wanted their Queen—the same monarch who led them each year with such dignity and solemn sadness on Remembrance

Day—to suddenly react as they were reacting, or as they might imagine the more emotionally transparent Diana to react. Putting aside all the family baggage and the emotional friction of Charles and Diana's divorce, the public's demand was still unreasonable. What they wanted would be incredibly out of character for their Queen under any circumstances.

Instead of joining her subjects in a dramatic, or melodramatic, expression of public mourning, Queen Elizabeth focused on her family, particularly her two grandsons who had just lost their mother. If she had rushed to London to lead public mourning, then critics would have accused her of abandoning her grieving grandchildren in favor of photo ops at Buckingham Palace. Throughout her reign, the Queen had been criticized publicly for placing her duty above her family, but in a moment of crisis when she rightfully placed family first, public sentiment, clouded by grief, grew fickle.

The dilemma showcases the demands placed on a sovereign trying to maintain the past and adapt to the present. As theologian and royal historian Ian Bradley observes, "The Queen's response in remaining in seclusion at Balmoral with the two young princes . . . was in keeping with the dignified and reserved style of mourning which had long characterized British royalty. Yet it was widely interpreted as unfeeling and heartless by the tabloid press which shrieked at the Queen 'Show us you care' and 'Speak to us, Ma'am.'"[7]

One of the greatest points of contention involved the flagpole outside Buckingham Palace. For centuries, the only flag ever flown there was the reigning monarch's, and only then when he or she was in residence. Otherwise, the flagpole remained bare. No flag was ever flown at half-staff because when one monarch's reign ended, the successor's unique banner, known as the Royal Standard and often featuring their coat of arms, would go up in place of the previous one. Simply put, the Palace flagpole symbolized the unbroken continuity of their nation's monarchy.

In light of Diana's death, however, the media directed public attention to the vacant flagpole and made it a lightning rod for royal indifference. They insisted that flying a flag at half-staff was the worldwide protocol, as wearing a black armband had been for their grandparents, to signify their state of mourning to the world. The distinctly British tradition and royal history of the flagpole at Buckingham Palace suddenly meant nothing to the subjects it served, eclipsed by their populist perception.

From the Queen's point of view and that of the Royal Family, the demand must have seemed absurd, as illogical as a non sequitur. Royal advisers, led by the Queen's private secretary Robin Janvrin, urged Her Majesty to consider flying the Union Jack at half-staff as a kind of compromise. In a job inherently reliant on symbolism, Her Majesty had to choose whether to redefine many of the symbols foundational to the monarchy.

As the political pressure from new Prime Minister Tony Blair compounded the public outcry, the Queen's institutional staff as well as her own family (including her husband and mother) counseled her to maintain her silence. As a result, grief over the unexpected death of Diana—herself a vibrant symbol of a new, younger kind of royal, one perceived to be more in touch with her public—became angry and petulant.

Queen Elizabeth II is greeted by the Lord Lieutenant of Greater London, Kenneth Olisa, as she arrives at Scripture Union's 150th Anniversary Service of Celebration at St. Mary's Church, Islington, London, on December 6, 2017.

Scripture Union's 150th Anniversary Service of Celebration.

The archbishop of Canterbury placing St. Edward's Crown on the Queen, Westminster Abbey, London, June 2, 1953.

Her Majesty prepares to record her first Christmas broadcast while in Auckland, New Zealand, 1953.

Queen Elizabeth with one of her favorite corgis, 1969.

Her Majesty the Queen meets with students at the Royal School, established by Queen Victoria for children of families in the monarch's service, 2002.

Princess Elizabeth and Princess Margaret out with their corgi, 1943.

Joan Williams/Shutterstock

Tim Rooke/Shutterstock

Shutterstock

Queen Elizabeth at the multifaith reception to commemorate Her Majesty's Diamond Jubilee, Lambeth Palace, London, February 12, 2012.

The hearse bearing the Queen Mother arrives at Windsor Castle, April 4, 2002.

King George VI in his Royal Naval uniform, 1944.

Formal portrait of Queen Victoria at the time of her Golden Jubilee in 1887.

Her Majesty the Queen presents Mother Teresa with the Order of Merit, November 24, 1983.

Delivering her 2002 Christmas broadcast, Queen Elizabeth reflects on the previous fifty years of her reign.

The final voyage of the Royal Yacht *Britannia*, Hong Kong, 1997.

Her Majesty the Queen and Prince Philip, the Duke of Edinburgh, celebrating their fiftieth wedding anniversary, Westminster Abbey, 1997.

The official wedding portrait of Her Majesty the Queen, then Princess Elizabeth, and Prince Philip, Westminster Abbey, London, November 20, 1947.

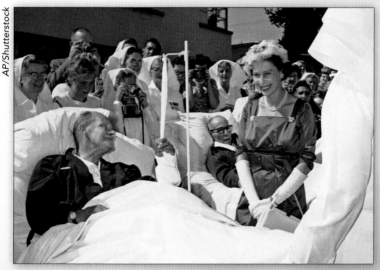

Queen Elizabeth visits wounded veterans at the Veterans' Hospital, Victoria, Canada, 1959.

Princess Elizabeth (center of top row) served in the Auxiliary Territorial Service, the women's branch of the British Army during World War II, 1939.

Artist Ralph Heimans stands beside his painting of Queen Elizabeth II inside the Chapter House at Westminster Abbey on May 17, 2013.

Public opinion polls on the monarchy plunged to all-time lows, indicating it should be dissolved or replaced.

Queen Elizabeth was understandably distressed by such backlash, not for herself personally, most likely, but for the monarchy itself. To fulfill her role as her subjects' leader in a time of national crisis, she would have to redefine how she carried out her responsibilities. Simply put, there is a time to follow rules and a time to break them, and wisdom lies in knowing the difference. Queen Elizabeth possessed the wisdom necessary to adapt to change. The loss of Diana had highlighted an epic sea change in British culture, a movement from reserve and privacy to self-expression, transparency, and accessibility. As a result, the Queen realized she would need to serve her subjects as a voice for their collective loss.

When the Queen finally returned to London and examined the thousands of bouquets and mementos mourners had left at the gates of Buckingham Palace, the palpable tension had reached its point. As Her Majesty and the Duke of Edinburgh approached the floral tributes, the crowd clapped. As she spoke with some individuals in the swollen crowd mourning Diana, their mood embraced her attention. The Queen became the comforter they needed, as much mother as monarch for the populist throng looking for solace. She asked people how they were doing, how long they had waited to sign the remembrance books, and thanked them for coming during her family's time of loss.

One of the most poignant moments of that occasion, included in the film *The Queen*, occurred when a little girl held out a fresh bouquet for Her Majesty. "Would you like me to place them for you?" the Queen asked. "No, Your Majesty," the girl replied. "They're for you."[8]

That evening, Queen Elizabeth delivered an address broadcast live, eulogizing Diana and praising her "capacity to smile and laugh" and "to inspire others with her warmth and kindness." Her speech reflected both the personal and the public roles she had balanced that week, as both queen and grandmother. She acknowledged her respect and admiration for Diana's "energy and commitment to others" as well as "her devotion to her two boys."[9] With compassion, dignity, and a gracious respect for the woman who, in life, had consistently challenged every dimension of the monarchy, the Queen voiced the grief of her family, her country, the Commonwealth, and the world.

The following day, when Queen Elizabeth left Buckingham Palace to attend the funeral of her former daughter-in-law at Westminster Abbey, the Union Jack flapped in a misty breeze, lowered to half-staff on the Palace flagpole for the first time in the history of the British monarchy.

The death of Princess Diana was not the only time Queen Elizabeth adapted her role as monarch to accommodate unprecedented expressions of grief. Decades earlier, after the assassination of US President John F. Kennedy, Queen Elizabeth treated the loss with exceptional respect and the kind of national display of grief reserved for members of the Royal Family. The tenor bell at Westminster Abbey was rung every minute between 11:00 a.m. and noon on the day after Kennedy's death, and royal residences continued to follow mourning protocol for one week in honor of him. A service of prayer for Kennedy's peaceful repose was also held at

Westminster Cathedral, the mother church of the Catholic Church in Great Britain.

Almost forty years after Kennedy's death, and four years after Diana's passing, Queen Elizabeth responded to another US tragedy with a depth of caring transcending historical precedent and British tradition. In the wake of terrorist attacks in the United States on September 11, 2001, the Queen spoke for her entire nation as well as the Commonwealth when she noted her "disbelief and total shock" over such egregious acts, which included the loss of nearly three thousand people after commercial planes crashed into the Twin Towers.[10]

In the days immediately after the terrorist attacks, Queen Elizabeth boldly broke royal tradition by authorizing the Royal Regimental Band to play "The Star-Spangled Banner" during the Changing of the Guard at Buckingham Palace rather than the customary British national anthem. Thousands of US citizens, along with many sympathetic Britons, wept openly as they held their right hands over their hearts during the iconic ceremony.

Queen Elizabeth also prepared a message to be read on her behalf at a memorial service held the following week at Saint Thomas Church, an Episcopal congregation on Fifth Avenue in New York City. The prayer service honored the British citizens whose lives were lost in the terrorist attacks, and the British ambassador to the US, Sir Christopher Meyer, read the Queen's heartfelt address, in equal parts lament and encouragement. Her Majesty wrote:

> Each and every one of us has been shocked and numbed by what we have witnessed in these recent days. But

none of us should doubt the resilience and determination of this great and much loved city and its people. Men and women from many nations, from many faiths and from many backgrounds were working together in New York City when this unimaginable outrage overtook them all. . . . My thoughts and my prayers are with you all now and in the difficult days ahead. But nothing that can be said can begin to take away the anguish and the pain of these moments. Grief is the price we pay for love.[11]

Years later, during a visit to New York to address the UN in 2010, Queen Elizabeth visited Ground Zero and paid her respects to those who died as part of the attacks on 9/11. She placed a wreath at the memorial there and opened an onsite garden honoring the sixty-seven British lives lost there at the site of the former World Trade Center. Chatting with those in attendance, the Queen told Debbie Palmer, the widow of a New York battalion fire chief who lost his life that fateful day, that she had never seen anything as shocking as the atrocity in 2001. Considering the devastation she witnessed in World War II during the Blitz, not to mention terrorist attacks in her own country, Her Majesty made a dramatic point.[12]

More recently, Queen Elizabeth comforted individuals as well as her nation in the wake of the devastation caused by the Grenfell Tower fire, which claimed seventy-two lives in June 2017, the worst residential conflagration in London since World War II. The fire started when a refrigerator-freezer malfunctioned in a fourth-story apartment, creating a blaze that quickly shot up the twenty-four-story building's exterior. Constructed in 1974 to provide council housing, Grenfell Tower consisted of 129 apartments that could shelter about six hundred residents. When the fire broke out shortly after midnight, only about 350 residents called Grenfell their home.

While the majority escaped harm, others could not overcome the smoke and heat trapping them in the boxlike tower, which had needed safety upgrades for some time. Similar to other tower blocks providing public housing in the UK, Grenfell followed a "stay put policy" in the event of fire. Thick walls and metal fire doors would supposedly contain a fire in any one part of the tower from spreading to the rest, enabling firefighters to arrest it. This design assumed that a full evacuation of all residents would never be necessary; therefore, the tower had no central fire alarm system or main exit strategy.

Although two fire engines arrived six minutes after being alerted by the fourth-story resident with the faulty freezer, the tower burned for almost sixty hours before being extinguished. By that time more than 250 firefighters and 70 fire engines had been enlisted to battle the inferno. More than 100 ambulance service crew members ministered medical aid onsite while about 20 ambulances transported residents to hospitals and clinics for treatment of burns and smoke inhalation. Dozens of paramedics, police officers, and members of London's Hazardous Area Response Team also assisted in efforts to rescue and treat Grenfell residents.

Queen Elizabeth wasted no time issuing a statement in response to the tragedy:

My thoughts and prayers are with those families who have lost loved ones in the Grenfell Tower fire and the many people who are still critically ill in hospital. Prince Philip and I would like to pay tribute to the bravery of firefighters and other emergency services officers who put their own lives at risk to save others. It is also heartening to see the incredible generosity of community volunteers rallying to help those affected by this terrible event.[13]

The Queen also wasted no time in arranging to meet with surviving residents. Just two days after the deadly fire, Her Majesty and her grandson Prince William surprised survivors and volunteer personnel with a personal visit at the Westway Sports Centre, a makeshift shelter and aid center for residents and their families. Although covered widely in the media afterward, the visit had not been announced beforehand to make it clear that they were there to console and support victims, not to solicit attention to their benevolence. Their arrival was greeted with applause and gratitude, and the Queen and Prince William spent nearly an hour talking with individuals about the trauma they experienced.

Throughout those exchanges, the Queen appeared to be on the verge of tears as she listened to survivors describe the anguished screams of those unable to escape the burning building. Even though they escaped with their lives, most survivors were faced with starting their lives over from nothing. Prince William also clearly became emotional as he listened intently to the tragic stories. A lifelong advocate for mental health, His Royal Highness emphasized the importance of counseling, promising to make sure resources were available for emotional and psychological follow-up.

Before departing, the Queen and Prince William signed a book of condolence. They also spoke with volunteers providing clothing, food, and temporary accommodations for survivors and victims' families. Queen Elizabeth, then age ninety-one, has continued to make comforting her subjects an indisputable priority.

Their visit was not the only time the Royal Family met with survivors, as they have continued to support victims of the Grenfell Tower fire. Shortly after Prince Harry married American actress Meghan Markle in May 2018, the media discovered that the Duchess of Sussex, the newest member of the Royal Family, had regularly been meeting with victims' families and survivors discreetly over the previous year. How fitting, then, that the young Duchess, accompanying her new grandmother-in-law, Queen Elizabeth, on a visit to Cheshire, joined with countless others on the one-year anniversary of the Grenfell fire to observe a moment of silence.

Although perhaps she is more comfortable showing public grief now than earlier in her reign, Queen Elizabeth continues to show both her strength and her compassion in the way she comforts those in crisis. While a few critics of the monarchy continue to describe her as removed from the pain of ordinary citizens, the vast majority of her subjects seem to agree that "she has an almost unfailing instinct for the right word and gesture in times of crisis."[14]

As with other important Christian themes, the significance of comfort and compassion have often been emphasized in Queen Elizabeth's annual Christmas broadcasts. In 2000 she reflected on the role of faith in the new millennium, sharing, "For me the teachings of Christ and my own personal accountability before God provide a framework in which I try to lead my life. I, like so many of you, have drawn great comfort in difficult times from Christ's words and example."[15]

Queen Elizabeth not only draws comfort from Christ's words and example, she offers it to those around her. She exemplifies what it means to be a follower of Jesus: "[God] comforts us in all our troubles, so that we can comfort those in any trouble with the comfort we ourselves receive from God. For just as we share abundantly in the sufferings of Christ, so also our comfort abounds through Christ" (2 Corinthians 1:4–5). When she provides solace to others, Her Majesty shows that she understands what Jesus meant when he said, "Blessed are those who mourn, for they will be comforted" (Matthew 5:4).

Her profound observation that grief is the price we pay for love reflects the nature of God depicted throughout the Bible. Whether in his relationship with the people of Israel or in the longsuffering of a prodigal son's parent, God emerges as a compassionate Father, like a mother hen gathering her wayward chicks under her wing. "He heals the brokenhearted and binds up their wounds," proclaims the psalmist (Psalm 147:3), while the prophet Isaiah reassures,

> So do not fear, for I am with you;
>> do not be dismayed, for I am your God.
> I will strengthen you and help you;
>> I will uphold you with my righteous hand.
>
> *Isaiah 41:10*

As a naturally shy person in the most public of roles imaginable, Queen Elizabeth has overcome both her personal inhibitions as well as the imposed isolation of the monarchy to serve her subjects with leadership that gives voice to their greatest losses. Having suffered painful losses of her own—as a wife, a mother, a daughter, and a sister—she makes shared grief an opportunity for connection, a bridge uniting all people regardless of their differences. She has been willing to pay the price for love, showing others what it means to care in the face of devastating heartache.

"So, you're writing on Her Majesty's faith, are you?" one middle-aged British woman asked me, rather skeptically, after a Sunday church service as we sipped tea from china cups in the large fellowship hall. She and I had not been introduced, but in a small congregation I likely stood out as the conspicuous American guest of a member family well known and much beloved by the church and surrounding community. Ignoring her rather accusatory tone, I acknowledged the purpose of my visit and explained some of my findings thus far. She seemed visibly relieved to hear that my focus on the Queen's faith was intended to inspire readers.

With oval tortoise-shell glasses, tweed skirt and green cardigan, and dark blond hair fading to ivory, Sheila had the thoughtful manner of a teacher or librarian. She was likely in her fifties or sixties with a northern accent that identified her as a lifelong resident of this area near Manchester. "Her Majesty sets an example that most people ignore," she said. "They consider her faith as a security blanket for the absence of their own. For most young people today, faith is as outdated and nostalgic as the monarchy."

She paused to sip her tea before continuing. "Only, some of them are coming 'round to realize that believing in something greater than oneself is the only way to survive this life. That's why I believe the Queen is more popular than ever. We need hope in this world. We need faithful examples. We need strong leaders unafraid to show us how to persevere in the midst of life's tragedies."

"How has the Queen managed to set such an example?" I asked.

Sheila looked me up and down as if someone apparently so thick should not be writing a book on the monarch's faith. After a few moments of awkward silence, she concluded that my question was an invitation for her opinion rather than a lack of knowledge on my part.

"Well, goodness," she said, "just look at the list of calamities and crises since World War II. The Cold War. Suez. The eighties and Mrs. Thatcher. The Falklands. The peccadilloes of her children and their rather sordid personal lives. Princess Diana, of course. Lovely she was but . . . Your 9/11. The internet and all this social media claptrap. It's not all bad . . . I do hope you know what I mean? As the world spins off its axis, the Queen catches it and restores balance and order again. She's the good mother who can be firm and consistent, kind and loving in equal measure."

We chatted about a few of the big events and people she mentioned for a few moments before landing on the topic of grief.

"Have the Queen's personal losses changed the way she leads? Was Princess Diana's death a turning point?" I asked.

"No, luv," Sheila said. "There was no overnight turning point then. It's a matter of degrees, daily and imperceptible. As we grow older, well, one must choose, mustn't one? How will we love those around us, the way Jesus showed us to love, and still carry on with whatever we're called by duty to do? It requires suffering, doesn't it? No matter whether you're the Queen of England or a widowed pensioner like myself, you accept life as a slow parade of losing those you hold most dear. Or you can retreat from life and withdraw to one's own devices, but you miss the joy of the parade, then, don't you?"

Tears welled in my eyes as I absorbed the intimate wisdom being shared with me. I tried to smile and keep my emotion from showing, but Sheila recognized it nonetheless.

"Forgive me for blathering on!" she said, lightening the mood. "I must sound like quite the old mad woman, mustn't I?"

"You sound very wise," I said.

Sheila smiled back, and fine lines crinkled around her eyes. She may have been older than she appeared. Then she lightly placed her hand on mine and peered into my empty cup. "You need another cup of tea, luv!" A command, not a question.

I must have looked at her funny, a little sad to shift away from such a personal moment of connection. I nodded.

"Come on, then," she said. "Do us both a bit of good."

*Let us not take ourselves too
seriously. None of us has a
monopoly on wisdom.*

—*annual Christmas broadcast,
1991*

chapter nine

WIT *and* WISDOM

FINDING JOY BY
KEEPING PERSPECTIVE

When Nellie Williams was growing up, she and her brother attended a nursery school near Windsor, located about thirty miles outside London and, of course, the site of Queen Elizabeth's favorite residence. Each year in early June, Nellie and her classmates would enjoy an outing to nearby Windsor Great Park for a picnic and field day. Most times their trip coincided with the Queen's annual procession from Windsor Castle to the iconic Ascot Racecourse, less than seven miles away, during Royal Ascot week.

Led by riders in scarlet coats on white horses, the Royal Procession, as it's known, features Her Majesty and accompanying members of the Royal Family in horse-drawn landaus, a type of four-wheeled, convertible carriage. The timeless pageantry of the event never fails to thrill spectators lined along the route. Nellie later recalled the excitement she and all the children shared as they began waving, cheering, and twirling small Union Jacks as Her Majesty passed by them in the park: "I thought it was magical; all the children would be in their school uniforms with little red berets for the girls and little red caps for the boys."[1]

One summer when Nellie was around eight, she went to visit her grandparents in Bath, a small city in the Southwest often visited by tourists for its Roman-built therapeutic baths

dating back many centuries (and celebrated in literature by the Wife of Bath in Geoffrey Chaucer's *Canterbury Tales*). During Nellie's visit, Queen Elizabeth planned to stop in Bath as part of her Silver Jubilee Celebrations in 1977. Like most of Bath's residents, Nellie's family lined up in hopes of seeing the Queen, or better still, actually meeting her during her walkabout.

Donna Lightbown, seven years old, of Blackpool breaks ranks outside Preston Town Hall to present a rose to the Queen, June 20, 1977.
Peter Lomas/Daily Mail/Shutterstock

Nellie, along with her grandfather and brother, stood at the front of the crowded route as Her Majesty strolled along the Royal Crescent, meeting her subjects and greeting well-wishers. Wearing white gloves and shaking hands, her black handbag dangling from her arm, Queen Elizabeth smiled, nodded, and gave hellos along the promenade until she was only a few feet from young Nellie. Sure enough, the Queen then stopped to chat with Nellie's grandfather. Then it was her turn, and Nellie blurted out the burning question that had just popped into her mind. In a high-pitched squeak, she said, "I . . . I used to stand in Windsor Great Park and wave my red beret at you, do you remember me, do ya?"[2]

Her very proper grandfather and self-conscious brother were immediately consumed with embarrassment at Nellie's childishly naive question. But then, "with a lovely smile across her face," the Queen looked down and said, "Well, *yes*, I think I do!"[3]

Her royal encounter created an indelible memory for Nellie Williams. Reflecting on the moment as an adult many years later, she said, "The Queen was the most famous person in the world to me. And do you know, I don't know if she did or didn't recognize me that day, but she had the forethought to think that it would mean a lot to me, this eight-year-old girl in front of her. I have been a massive fan ever since. I'm glad I met her and I am glad I said what I said because her reply not only made my day but in my eyes it also made her human."[4]

No one could reign for over six decades and grow more beloved with each passing year without thinking quickly on their feet. Throughout her life in the public eye, Queen Elizabeth has embraced meeting her subjects, even when making the monarchy more accessible required her to step outside her royal comfort zone. At a young age, she understood the importance of connecting with other people and not allowing her privileged role and inherited titles to come between them. She has a curiosity about people, especially those who lead ordinary lives, which likely carries an edge of envy for the anonymity and privacy they enjoy, ordinary gifts Her Majesty has rarely known.

Queen Elizabeth also has a quick wit and sense of humor that has endeared her to many of her visitors. On average, the Queen hosts more than fifty thousand people each year at dinners, receptions, garden parties, luncheons, banquets, and teas—and this number reflects only the events at Buckingham Palace.[5] Including other state occasions and public events, the number of people the Queen meets each year easily exceeds one hundred thousand.

Despite the volume of introductions and encounters, Her Majesty makes considerable effort to connect with each person she meets. When possible, she requests background information on her guests to find areas of common interest. With members of the public, she usually focuses on general topics such as family, seasonal events, and the weather.

The Queen also knows that most people, even celebrities and world leaders, are often nervous when they meet her for the first time. Most are aware of the formal protocol involved in meeting Her Majesty and want to show her proper respect while also engaging in the opportunity of the present moment. When she enters the room, everyone must stand. New acquaintances wait to be introduced or for the Queen to initiate an introduction or greeting.

She is first addressed as "Your Majesty," which may then be followed by "Ma'am." Women traditionally curtsy, while men bow from the shoulders or nod from the neck. When walking, others naturally follow the Queen, who must always lead any procession or entrance. When departing from her presence, one must never turn their back on Her Majesty, which requires backing out of rooms, a feat that often results in stumbles or less-than-graceful exits. Because this practice is now considered a safety risk (especially for the elderly), its practice is limited to a few ceremonial occasions.

Her role, her personality, and her security all limit demonstrations of affection or physical interactions. No one is allowed to touch the Queen unless she offers a hand to shake. Then it is polite to respond in kind but only for a brief, light touch rather than a firm handshake. Considering how many people she meets each year, it's no wonder Her Majesty wears her famous white gloves, as much a health precaution as a royal fashion accessory.

On occasion, however, some individuals simply cannot contain their enthusiasm when meeting Queen Elizabeth. When she visited Washington, DC, in 1991, Her Majesty accompanied then-First Lady Barbara Bush to meet community leader Alice Frazier, a sixty-seven-year-old great-grandmother reclaiming her Marshall Heights neighborhood from gangs and drug dealers. Welcoming the famous women to her home, Mrs. Frazier immediately hugged them both, unaware of the breach of protocol and later saying, "It felt like the natural thing to do."[6] The Queen responded naturally and made no mention of the faux pas.

The following year, Australian Prime Minister Paul Keating put his arm around Queen Elizabeth during their meeting, resulting in numerous tabloid photos proclaiming Keating the "Lizard of Oz." His successor, John Howard, would repeat such a mistake when meeting the Queen, although his office later denied that he made any actual contact with Her Majesty.

In 2009, while attending the G-20 Summit in London, President Barack Obama and First Lady Michelle met Queen Elizabeth and Prince Philip in their private apartments at Buckingham Palace, where they got acquainted and exchanged gifts. Later that evening at a reception for Summit leaders, photographers snapped photos of Mrs. Obama hugging the Queen, who returned the warm gesture. They clearly enjoyed chatting and were seen laughing and smiling throughout the cordial exchange. When reporters later inquired about the First Lady's breach of protocol, the Palace responded, "It was a mutual and spontaneous display of affection. We don't issue instructions on not touching the Queen."[7]

Not all presidential affection is reciprocal, however. In 1977 President Jimmy Carter visited Buckingham Palace to attend a formal dinner for NATO leaders, pleased to share that it was his first time traveling outside the US. Greeting the Queen Mother, President Carter tried to charm the seventy-six-year-old royal by noting how much she reminded him of his own dear mother, "Miz Lillian." Then in a burst of spontaneous enthusiasm, he kissed the shocked Queen Mother on her lips! Later she recalled, "I took a sharp step backwards, but not quite far enough," adding that she had not been kissed like that since the death of her husband, King George VI.[8]

Queen Elizabeth likely enjoyed a laugh at her mother's expense that night because she regularly finds the humor in situations that go awry. The noted Labour Party leader and writer Richard Crossman once observed, "She laughs with her whole face and she cannot just assume a mere smile because she's really a very spontaneous person."[9] The Queen is known to enjoy jokes, gag gifts, and mimicking others' mannerisms and accents when sharing anecdotes. She doesn't mind laughing at her own expense, or giving as good as she gets.

President George W. Bush inadvertently brought out Her Majesty's good-natured humor in 2007 while welcoming her in an official ceremony on the White House lawn. Known for misspeaking in his warm Texas drawl, Bush mistakenly noted that the Queen had previously visited Washington in 1776—instead of 1976—to help celebrate the US Bicentennial. Correcting his mistake, the President then turned and winked at Queen Elizabeth before quipping, "She gave me a look that only a mother could give a child."[10]

Before her visit concluded, though, Queen Elizabeth got the last laugh. Speaking at a formal dinner hosted by the British ambassador, the Queen began by thanking President Bush and offering a toast in his honor. Grinning gleefully, she said, "I wondered whether I should start this toast by saying, 'When I was here in 1776 . . .'" Everyone roared with laughter, most of all, the President, who began his own speech that evening by noting, "Your Majesty, I can't top that one!"[11]

While entertaining guests at one of the royal residences, Queen Elizabeth often takes a hands-on approach, inspecting guest quarters, ensuring their comfort, and choosing a menu to their liking. When President Ronald Reagan and First Lady Nancy visited Windsor Castle in 1982 as personal guests, not as heads of state, the Queen went out of her way to make them feel welcome, including a dedicated White House telephone line and installation of showers in their en suite bathrooms, apparently a first for the over-nine-hundred-year-old property.[12]

During the Reagans' visit, the president, aware of the Queen's love of horses and riding, was keen to go horseback riding with Her Majesty. Happy to host such an experience for the ranch-owning Californian, Queen Elizabeth arranged an hour ride through eight miles of Windsor's Home Park, much of it following a canal running adjacent to the Thames River.

The two world leaders naturally attracted the attention of reporters and photographers eager to cover their leisurely excursion. Reagan, accustomed to always playing for the cameras, stopped frequently to smile and wave, likely to the Queen's displeasure because she typically enjoys her rides as time away from public scrutiny. Still, she had to smile when a reporter yelled at Reagan from behind the press barricade, "Does it ride well?" The President immediately stopped and cheerfully yelled back, "Yes! If you stand still, I'll take it over the top."[13]

Horseback riding isn't the only way the Queen enjoys guiding guests who visit one of the royal properties; she often drives them herself on a personal tour of the grounds. Reportedly, her driving style is as determined and no-nonsense as her personality. In fact, in 1998 when Crown Prince Abdullah of Saudi Arabia visited Her Majesty's Scottish estate, Balmoral, she asked whether he wanted a tour of the grounds after their luncheon. The Crown Prince gladly accepted the Queen's offer.

When he and his interpreter were seated in a Land Rover

that afternoon, the Saudi monarch did a double take when Queen Elizabeth herself got behind the wheel. In his country, government restrictions prohibit women from driving, so the Prince was understandably surprised. His surprise turned to alarm when the Queen floored the accelerator while driving on the narrow estate road. Not only that, but she frequently turned to him as she chatted away about various points of interest.

As their back-road journey continued, Abdullah apparently feared for his life and pleaded, through his interpreter, for Her Majesty to slow down and keep her eyes on the road. While she nodded and smiled each time the interpreter voiced the Prince's alarm, the Queen drove on, confident something must have gotten lost in translation.[14]

Unlike many members of her generation, Queen Elizabeth has quickly embraced technology. She was the first head of state to send an email, back in 1976. She waited until some of the virtual dust had settled, however, to join Facebook in 2010 with a page for "The British Monarchy." She also opened a twitter account, @BritishMonarchy, and sent her first tweet appropriately enough at the opening of a new exhibition on the information age at London's Science Museum.

The Queen naturally brings her sense of humor to the use of technology, enjoying YouTube videos that she often shares with her husband, children, and grandchildren. When she and Prince Philip toured Google's London headquarters in 2008, they enjoyed a "laughing baby" clip, causing the Queen to comment, "Amazing a child would laugh like that."[15]

Her Majesty also enjoys causing others to laugh, particularly when it comes to opportunities for photobombing. In 2013 the Queen visited the new BBC headquarters, touring its state-of-the-art broadcast facilities and meeting with various leaders, performers, and celebrities while there. During her visit, she couldn't help but grow curious when she observed a studio set behind a glass partition. As she stepped closer and closer, viewers of the BBC News's afternoon broadcast couldn't believe their eyes.

Looming behind and between news anchors Julian Worricker and Sophie Long was a regal woman wearing a bright turquoise coat and matching hat. BBC staff, obviously trained not to interrupt live broadcasts, threw caution to the wind and crowded around Queen Elizabeth as the news presenters made the surreal discovery of the royal presence over their shoulders.[16] The slight smile on her face made it clear that Her Majesty likely knew what she was doing.

Similarly, the following year the Queen was visiting Glasgow in honor of the Commonwealth Games being played there in 2014 when another irresistible photobomb opportunity presented itself. On that bright, sunny, summer afternoon, Australian hockey player Jayde Taylor stopped to snap a couple of selfies with teammate Brooke Peris. Gazing directly into their shot from behind a chain-link fence a few feet away, Queen Elizabeth had a mischievous twinkle in her eyes. Her bright lime green suit and feathered hat could not be missed, outshone only by her wide smile and knowing expression.[17]

Finding humor in daily affairs and exercising her sharp wit comes naturally to Queen Elizabeth, but from a young age she has also shown considerable maturity and wisdom. Her personality and temperament certainly contribute to both her wit and her wisdom, but strikingly enough, the source of her wisdom has remained consistent throughout her life. The Queen has made no secret of her reliance on the Bible as the primary source for her faith in Christ.

The Queen Mother instilled a great love of the Bible in her daughters when they were young, reading from the King James Version as well as having them memorize favorite passages, often from the Psalms. "People don't know that almost certainly every night the Queen kneels beside her bed and says her prayers because that is what her mother did, we know, and her grandmother before her, and that's how she was brought up," Robert Lacey, royal biographer and historical consultant for *The Crown*, has explained.[18]

The sacred authority of the Bible figured at the center of Elizabeth's coronation, where it was described as "the most valuable thing that this world affords."[19] From the beginning of her reign, the Queen has consistently cited references from the Bible, particularly in her annual Christmas broadcasts. "To what greater inspiration and counsel can we turn," she asked rhetorically, "than to the imperishable truth to be found in this treasure house, the Bible?"[20] In her 2016 address, Her Majesty explained, "Billions of people now follow Christ's teaching and find in him the guiding light for their lives. I am one of them because Christ's example helps me see the value in doing small things with great love, whoever does them and whatever they themselves believe."[21]

Another iconic follower of Jesus, Billy Graham, attested

to the Queen's love for the Bible, as well as the strength and depth of her Christian faith, in his autobiography, *Just As I Am*. "[The Queen's] official position has prevented her from openly endorsing our Crusade meetings," he wrote. "But by welcoming us and having me preach on several occasions to the royal family at Windsor and Sandringham, she has gone out of her way to be quietly supportive of our mission."[22]

After the *The Crown*'s "Vergangenheit," episode, many viewers expressed surprise at the depiction of the Queen's friendship with Reverend Graham, best known for his worldwide evangelical crusades, which is how he came to meet Queen Elizabeth while in London for such an event in 1955. In an interview after the episode's release, Peter Morgan explained, "The Billy Graham episode is about Elizabeth wanting to deepen her Christianity. She stops reflecting on forgiveness as a central tenet of Christianity at precisely the time that she's asked whether she can or can't forgive her uncle [David, the Duke of Windsor, who reigned as King Edward VIII until his abdication]."

As shown in that episode and according to factual documents and historical photographs, her uncle met secretly with Nazis, including Adolf Hitler, and seemed to hold a favorable disposition toward them, even after Britain entered World War II. Deeply troubled by these revelations, Queen Elizabeth struggled to forgive her uncle despite wanting to make peace and unite her family. Whether or not she expressly asked Reverend Graham for his counsel remains unknown but is certainly feasible. Morgan said, "The two story themes dovetail quite nicely. It's the best bit of writing in the season."[23]

Over the decades that followed, the Queen and Graham remained friends. In his autobiography, Graham wrote, "No one in Britain has been more cordial toward us than Her Majesty Queen Elizabeth II. Almost every occasion I have been with her has been in a warm, informal setting, such as a luncheon or dinner, either alone or with a few family members or other close friends."[24] They rarely publicized their meetings or leveraged their relationship professionally, but the two clearly enjoyed a friendship that endured for over sixty years until Reverend Graham's passing in 2018.

Graham frequently praised his royal friend's intelligence and wisdom, calling her "unquestionably one of the best-informed people on world affairs I have ever met."[25] During private conversations, the two often discussed sermon topics and various passages from the Bible. Graham recalled visiting the Queen while traveling through Great Britain during the Christmas season. In preparation for her annual Christmas Day broadcast, the Queen was writing her address and asked for Graham's input. Apparently, she wanted to include a visual aid for one of her main points by tossing a stone into a pond to show how the ripples expanded from its impact.

On another occasion, Graham returned the favor and asked for Queen Elizabeth's opinion on his sermon topic and related Scripture. He had just finished preaching at Windsor one Sunday at the Queen's invitation, followed by lunch. Seated next to Her Majesty, Graham shared that he had been undecided about what to preach on until the last moment and "had almost preached on the healing of the crippled man in John 5." The Queen instantly got excited and exclaimed,

"I wish you had! That is my favorite story."[26] Graham wasn't surprised by her reaction and concluded, "Her eyes sparkled and she bubbled over with enthusiasm, as she could do on occasion. I always found her very interested in the Bible and its message."[27]

Queen Elizabeth is indeed interested in the Bible and is committed to sharing its gospel message. In fact, she gladly agreed to participate in the publication of a special book to commemorate her ninetieth birthday entitled *The Servant Queen and the King She Serves*. While she often references her faith in her Christmas broadcasts and speeches, the Queen rarely writes about her personal beliefs or endorses explicitly Christian publications, making that project all the more remarkable.

This overview of Her Majesty's Christian faith was published by Bible Society UK, for whom the Queen serves as patron, along with HOPE and the London Institute for Contemporary Christianity. Her Majesty personally wrote the foreword, describing how touched she was by the project but also thanking readers for their prayers and good wishes. She wrote, "I have been—and remain—very grateful to . . . God for His steadfast love. I have indeed seen His faithfulness."[28]

The book was distributed to thousands of churches across the UK and throughout many Commonwealth countries prior to the Queen's official ninetieth birthday celebration in 2016, an event that included a dynamic street party with more than ten thousand participants crowding the Mall outside Buckingham Palace. In honor of Her Majesty's stalwart faith, churches across the nation and around the world were encouraged to plan and host celebrations of their own.

At hundreds, if not thousands, of such church-sponsored parties, over 100,000 copies of *The Servant Queen and the King She Serves* were given away and used as faith-based conversation starters in local communities. The book proved so popular that the Bible Society had to print another 150,000 copies to meet demand. While so many beloved leaders celebrate personal milestones with philanthropy and public service, it's hard to imagine a more fitting way to celebrate than this.

Because of her example for more than half a century, such a remarkable project as *The Servant Queen* should not surprise us. Whether meeting gleeful school children such as young Nellie Williams or demonstrative admirers such as Michelle Obama, Queen Elizabeth freely shares her warmth, wit, and wily humor. In equal measure she also reveals her wisdom and invests it in a timeless legacy for future generations. Her Majesty embodies Christ's instruction to be both "wise as serpents" and also "innocent as doves" (Matthew 10:16 ESV). She uses both to keep perspective on her life even as she inspires us all to do the same.

Covent Garden is one of my favorite places in all of London. Located in the West End, it covers several city blocks that loosely frame the Covent Garden Piazza, a pedestrian-only shopping and dining district. Mostly brick and cobblestone, the market square remains a favorite for tourists and locals alike, built on and around the area where fruits and vegetables were sold in open-air markets dating back centuries.

On my first trip to London over thirty years ago, Covent Garden reminded me of Greenwich Village in New York, creative and free-spirited, urban and artistic, and a little bohemian. Little boutiques and one-of-a-kind artisan shops were nestled next to pubs and cafés while buskers performed and street merchants offered handmade jewelry, scarves, trinkets, and souvenirs. I've visited it at least half a dozen times since then, and while it's become more upscale and touristy, it still retains some of its free-spirited appeal.

During my most recent visit, I took the Piccadilly line on the tube to visit my favorite pipe tobacco store, Segar and Snuff Parlour, a tiny shop in Covent Garden's Market Building. With its entrance guarded by a life-size Highlander statue, the small space reveals an expansive, timeless sense of past traditions. The shop carries all kinds of smoking-related paraphernalia, but I'm always entranced by its rich, sweet tobacco smell and surprisingly wide selection of English pipes.

The day had started out typically dreary, but shortly after lunch the sun dispelled the cloud cover as if slowly lifting the lid off a closed pot. Christmas shoppers and tourists filled narrow sidewalks as I made my way from the tube station to the Piazza. Approaching the Market Building, I couldn't resist snapping a few pictures of the holiday decorations: fresh evergreens, holly branches, Victorian-looking ornaments, and twinkling white lights. Street vendors offered every gift imaginable: T-shirts and scarves, perfume and purses, earrings and bracelets, sunglasses and umbrellas, biscuits and sweets. And, of course, royal souvenirs, with the newlyweds the Duke and Duchess of Sussex the most popular by far.

Some of the proprietors acted reserved and polite toward shoppers, while others honed their best pitches like carnival barkers. Browsing at a corner table filled with neatly displayed rows of royal teacups, mugs, wedding programs, photo books, key rings, and Christmas ornaments, I must have looked like an easy sell to the young man reigning over these displays.

"Hiya, mate," he said with a lopsided grin. "Out doin' yer holiday shoppin', are ya? Well, you've come to the right place! Lots of choice mementos from your time in London for that special someone. What catches yer eye here?"

His Cockney accent sounded a bit exaggerated, but I had to smile at his well-rehearsed patter. Wearing an oversized long-sleeved black T-shirt, faded denim jacket, and jeans torn at the knee on his thin, wiry frame, he resembled an urban scarecrow. His olive complexion, dark eyes, and black disheveled hair gave him an exotic charisma, reminding me of recent Academy Award–winning American actor Rami Malek.

"I'm not sure yet," I said politely. "What's your bestseller?"

My question seemed to surprise him. "You Canadian? Or from the States? Must be the States," he said as he looked me over. "I'm guessing posh American businessman here for very important meetings with Her Majesty the Queen—am I right?"

I laughed and slowly shook my head. "That obvious, is it?"

"Yeah, you got that royal look about ya!"

"Well, I am writing a book about her," I said, instantly wishing I hadn't.

"Are you, now?" He tilted his head and gave me that lopsided grin again. When I didn't respond, he said, "You really are, aren't you? I thought you were just taking the p—" A woman standing near the far side of his table interrupted to ask the price for a Union Jack–patterned tea cozy. He told her and took the five-pound note she handed him.

"It's a livin'," he said and shrugged. "Now, where were we, Lord Byron? Ah, yeah, a prince like you needs some palace swag to take home! Just look at those lovebirds, Harry and Megs! You won't find Royal Doulton teacups like 'ese in Buckingham Palace!" He reached behind him and held up a pale blue cup and saucer with a tasteful *H* and *M* monogram in gold. Compared with tea cozies and calendars, this was clearly one of his classier items, which I took as a kind of compliment.

"How much?" I asked, not needing or wanting the cup and saucer but already feeling obligated to buy something. Probably that Lord Byron crack did it.

"Well, for an entire set of eight, I'll make it simple— hundred quid, neat and clean." He pretended to take a sip from the cup, pinky extended and eyebrow cocked, before handing the saucer to me and resting the cup back in it.

"Where do you get these?" I asked, surprised that it did indeed bear the Royal Doulton imprimatur.

"Ask me no questions, and I'll tell you no lies!" he said and winked.

I had to laugh again, thinking I should just walk away. He must have sensed he was losing me and quickly said, "They're totally legit, mate. For just the one, wrapped up for transport back home, I'd need just one o' them twenty-pound notes burning a hole in your pocket."

I studied his eyes, deliberating on whether to haggle with him. "Hmm, maybe," I said. "Other than being good for business, what do you think of the Queen and Royal Family?" If I was going to buy something I didn't need, I might as well get something out of it.

"Aye, she's a bit all right, she is," Rami said. "Not sold on the rest of that lot. I'm bustin' it to scrape by, and they're in the dosh. Lots of busy, but any real work get done? You tell me. Must be nice, mustn't it?" Then he seemed to catch himself, realizing he was giving me his real opinion as opposed to what he thought I wanted to hear, what would be good for business. He looked around as if wondering who might have overheard him before saying, "Just windin' ya up, mate! They're my crew! Loves me some royals!"

I handed him a twenty-pound note and watched his eyes light up. I should have haggled. He produced a piece of bubble wrap like a magician conjuring a scarf and wrapped the china. "There ya go—cheers, mate!" I thanked him and turned, about to walk away and find Segar and Snuff, when he said, "Lord Byron, you really writin' a book on the Queen?"

There was no way I could resist.

"Ask me no questions, and I'll tell you no lies!"

Today we need a special kind of courage.
Not the kind needed in battle, but a kind which
makes us stand up for everything that we know
is right, everything that is true and honest.
We need the kind of courage that can withstand
the subtle corruption of the cynics, so that we
can show the world that we are
not afraid of the future.

—*annual Christmas broadcast,*
1957

chapter ten

MYSTERY *and* MAJESTY

ENDOWING A LEGACY OF FAITH
FOR FUTURE GENERATIONS

*I*n many ways, it was a Thursday afternoon in June like any other on a busy workday in London. Tim Haries, a forty-one-year-old electrician and father of two from South Yorkshire, wandered in to historic Westminster Abbey shortly after noon, easily blending in with visiting tourists and local workers on their lunch breaks. Strolling toward the East Cloister, Haries appeared in no hurry, although he definitely had a specific destination in mind: the Chapter House.

Originally used in the thirteenth century as a daily meeting place for monks to gather and "hold chapter" (pray, read, discuss), the octagonal room likely impressed Haries with its tiered seating, imposing central pillar, vaulted ceiling, and wall murals depicting biblical scenes such as the annunciation and the last judgment. Even more impressive was the focus of his visit, an oil painting measuring eight feet by eleven feet, newly installed just three weeks prior. As his work boots thudded across the medieval tiles covering the floor, Haries stared at the subject of the enormous portrait.

A handful of viewers murmured their approval, exiting as Haries anchored himself a few feet in front of the massive canvas. Haries read the plaque posted beside the grand painting: "*The Coronation Theatre: A Portrait of Her Majesty Queen Elizabeth II* by Ralph Heimans." According to the annotation, it had been unveiled the previous year, 2012, to commemorate the Queen's Diamond Jubilee, a year-long celebration of Her Majesty's sixty years on the throne.

Haries studied the painting, intrigued as thousands of other viewers were by the way the Australian artist depicted the Queen standing in the Sacrarium of Westminster Abbey, the so-called Coronation Theatre, on the thirteenth-century Cosmati pavement. It was the sacred stage where Elizabeth had made her coronation vows and been anointed sovereign six decades earlier, the same spot where virtually every monarch preceding her had enacted the same ceremony for nine hundred years. Wearing official State Dress, including the crimson velvet Robe of State that had draped her shoulders at her Coronation in 1953, the Queen appears lost in thought, perhaps contemplating all that has occurred since that momentous day.

Hearing voices echoing toward him, Haries knew he had to act fast to fulfill his mission. He reached into the ample pocket of his baggy workman's pants and produced the weapon he had managed to smuggle past security when he entered. His calloused hands snapped the plastic top off the small canister, and using only the power of his index finger, he did the unthinkable. Tim Haries spray-painted "help" in lowercase letters as large as he could make them across the standing figure of Her Majesty Queen Elizabeth II.[1]

Almost two years prior to that moment, the Queen had met with Mr. Heimans, a renowned contemporary portrait artist commissioned by the Jubilee committee to create a portrait of Her Majesty. She agreed to sit for an hour to provide Heimans with sketches he would then use to create his imaginary scene set in the abbey for *The Coronation Theatre.* "Through the narrative of the portrait," the artist explained, "I wanted to produce a work of particular significance for the Diamond Jubilee. By representing the Queen as she reflects on this incredible milestone in her life, I wanted to explore the dynamic between her public role and the personal, emotional dimension."[2]

After being unveiled to commemorate the Diamond Jubilee, the painting was displayed in the National Portrait Gallery in Canberra, Australia, for the rest of that year. When the painting returned to London in March 2013, it was purchased for placement in Westminster Abbey by Lord and Lady Harris of Peckham. While not unprecedented, the acquisition was noteworthy because the Abbey rarely places new works of art within its storied walls.

It's also worth noting that Westminster Abbey, once a Benedictine monastic cathedral in the sixteenth century, carries the unique status of "Royal Peculiar," meaning it is a church directly responsible to the sovereign. Combining these two facts, it seems highly likely that Queen Elizabeth approves of the portrait. As the subject of thousands of portraits, both official and personal, Her Majesty never comments on the finished works but sometimes reveals her approval in more subtle ways.

All of which made Tim Haries's act of vandalism even more shocking. Haries had hoped to attract attention on behalf of Fathers4Justice, a nonprofit group advocating for the rights of divorced and separated fathers. While a spokesman for the group immediately asserted that Mr. Haries acted alone and not on behalf of the organization, the act of vandalism echoed many of the attention-getting stunts members of Fathers4Justice have employed over the years, including naked protests, flour bombs, and scaling the Royal Courts of Justice building while dressed as Batman and Robin.[3]

No official statement was made from Buckingham Palace, but Lord Harris, the Abbey's benefactor, found the brazen defacement "ridiculous," while the artist, Mr. Heimans, simply called it "shocking."[4] Fortunately, most of the damage could be undone with the help of restoration experts and the artist. Originally expected to take around ten to twelve weeks, *The Coronation Theatre*'s restoration went smoothly, and the painting was reinstalled in Westminster Abbey in only a month. For the foreseeable future, it resides in the Queen's Diamond Jubilee Galleries under heightened security.

As Queen Elizabeth II approaches seventy years on the throne and a hundred years of life, the painting captures the bittersweet essence of a royal life well lived. Among so many kings and queens, poets and writers, the hallowed halls of this ancient Abbey seem a fitting home for this larger-than-life portrait of Britain's longest-reigning monarch. The artist said, "I could not have imagined a more fitting home for my portrait of the Queen than Westminster Abbey, the beauty of which was a great source of inspiration in the conception of the work. . . . The portrait's narrative will have its strongest resonance in this remarkable setting."[5]

This painting and incident of vandalism might well serve as a metaphor for the life and reign—the two are now almost synonymous—of Her Majesty Queen Elizabeth II. She has now gone the distance and proven herself to be a leader unlike any other. As depicted in Heimans's Diamond Jubilee portrait, the Queen has come full circle. At its first installation, the Dean of Westminster, The Very Reverend Dr. John Hall, described how the painting "speaks powerfully of the moment of Her Majesty's anointing and coronation sixty years ago . . . The Queen in the glorious space of the Abbey standing at the very place where she committed herself to God and her people reflects powerfully on the years of service."[6]

Set in the shadows of the Abbey, presumably at night, the portrait also conveys the solitary nature of the monarchy. The Queen's expression is meditative, reflective, almost wistful in its sense of remembering what took place on that very spot when she was just a twenty-six-year-old young woman at the dawn of a remarkable reign. An internal drama of emotions competes with the dramatic ceremony taking place around her. The joy, the fear, the anticipation, the uncertainty, the responsibility.

She could have no idea then of all that would transpire—with her family, her subjects, her nation, the Commonwealth, and the world at large. Unimaginable changes. Unrelenting pressure. Unbearable losses. She could not have foreseen the twists and turns of a role that by turns would require her to be both Sphinx and Oracle, a living symbol of the historic past, building a bridge to revelations of an unknown future.

The painting also expresses a paradox of past and present

in its setting, the mirrored duality of its subject standing in the ancient church in which the portrait now resides. Church and theater, altar and stage, crown and prop. With her center-stage role in history's great pageant now drawing to a close, the Queen's performance is almost complete. Only, it is not a performance, not artifice but sacrifice, an authentic life lived in fulfillment of a sacred vow between her and God.

No act of destruction, least of all a vandal's smear of acrylic spray paint, can tarnish the legacy of the woman whom God selected to be Queen. Any change in perception of her historic reign will only be a patina of nostalgic appreciation and abiding gratitude. How fitting as well as ironic that Mr. Haries chose the word *help* in defacing the Queen's portrait. Because that is exactly what she has been providing in one form or another for more than sixty years.

As *The Coronation Theatre* reminds us, Queen Elizabeth has established a legacy built on years of dedicated service. Her tireless efforts as patron of hundreds of charities, nonprofits, and worthwhile causes exceed those of any other British monarch in history. Even as she scales back her calendar and hands off many of her official duties—she is in her nineties, after all—the Queen continues to work more than forty hours each week.

Every day except for Christmas and Easter, she reviews the red box of documents and briefings submitted by the prime minister's office, key departments, and security services. Addressed as "Reader No. 1," the Queen reads each item carefully and often makes notations, asks questions, or offers counsel when requested. She meets weekly with the prime minister and undoubtedly shares her observations based on her keen intelligence and decades of experience.

Young Queen Elizabeth reading documents from the famous Red Box, circa 1956.
Universal History Archive/Getty Images

In addition to her responsibilities as head of state, the Queen signs off on hundreds of written documents each week—memos, plans, and official forms as well as both formal and personal correspondence. Her travel schedule remains legendary, even as she continues to reduce and simplify the number of trips she now takes. Simply traveling among the various royal residences and hosting the traditional, annual events that have become entrenched in her calendar would exhaust most people half her age.

She employs more than a thousand people but still feeds her own dogs most days. She attends church weekly, even during summer and Christmas holidays, and prays daily.

She interacts with hundreds of people on any given day and remains patient and gracious in virtually any situation. Political commentator Andrew Marr observed, "There are no reliable recorded incidents of the Queen losing her temper, using bad language, or refusing to carry out a duty expected of her."[7]

Queen Elizabeth is without a doubt the most famous woman in the world, but she remains her authentic, down-to-earth regal self whether visiting with children in a school, executives around a boardroom, workers in a factory, or heads of state at a palace banquet. She can ride her Fell pony for hours across the desolate beauty of the Highland moors as well as stay on her feet for even longer when touring Commonwealth nations or enjoying walkabouts among her subjects. No matter what setting or role she's in, however, the Queen relies on her faith in God to guide her.

As she now enters the twilight of her historic reign, the Queen has not only established an eternal legacy of gratitude, compassion, and service, she has invested in those who will follow her to ensure that their inheritance of those values is well spent. While most people in a family business choose successors to maintain the firm, Queen Elizabeth has instilled in her heirs, Prince Charles and his son Prince William, a sense of the mystery and majesty inherent to the monarchy.

In recent years, her intentional strategy for succession shows that she is not content to preserve what she has established but wants to see it grow and thrive. The Queen has never been one to rest on her laurels. Her example shows that spiritual faith is not the embalming fluid of one's legacy but its lifeblood.

The extent of the Queen's investment in her succession recently came to light on a world stage. While royal-watchers celebrated the wedding of Prince Harry to Meghan Markle in May 2018, many overlooked a momentous event for the monarchy the previous month. During the third week in April that year, heads of government from across fifty-three member nations had gathered in London for the Commonwealth Heads of Government Meeting (CHOGM). Comprised of both advanced and developing nations, with virtually all tied to the previous globe-spanning British Empire, the Commonwealth unites over two billion people from various parts of the world to advance shared goals, develop issue-related policies, and trade best practices.

The CHOGM is usually held every two years, rotating locations among members, with the previous conference in 2015 hosted by Valletta, Malta. The Pacific island of Vanuatu had been scheduled to host in 2017 but had to cancel in the wake of Cyclone Pam. With the Queen's blessing, British leaders offered to host in London instead, footing the more than $10-million cost and promising the largest intergovernmental summit ever held in the United Kingdom.

Because Queen Elizabeth had already announced that she would no longer travel abroad, leaders in the Commonwealth were grateful for another opportunity to meet with Her Majesty at what may have been her final CHOGM attended in person. Like many of her royal duties and responsibilities, leading these international summits will most likely be passed on to her heir, Prince Charles, when it next convenes. Welcoming other Commonwealth leaders, Prince Charles described the network of nations as "a fundamental feature of my life for as long as I can remember" and praised the many "strong and affectionate bonds" shared by its members.[8]

The Queen's opening address at Buckingham Palace echoed her son's and formally launched the week's activities. It was only fitting that she formally open the meeting since the "flourishing network," as she described it, has thrived largely because of her indomitable leadership, irrepressible charm, and personal engagement with each member nation's leaders. Many historians and political commentators believe the Commonwealth would not exist, let alone flourish, if not for Queen Elizabeth's steady presence.

She has headed the Commonwealth since 1952 after assuming the role from her father. In this capacity, the Queen presides over the summit meetings but does not participate in the Commonwealth leaders' discussions. Unlike the monarchy itself, the position is not hereditary, with leaders of member nations selecting each successor. With this fact in mind, the Queen made a direct request of those assembled: "It is my sincere wish that the Commonwealth will continue to offer stability and continuity for future generations and will decide that one day the Prince of Wales should carry on the important work started by my father in 1949."[9]

Her Majesty clearly had the future in mind as she concluded, "By continuing to treasure and reinvigorate our association and activities, I believe we will secure a safer, more prosperous and sustainable world for those who follow us, a world where the Commonwealth's generosity of spirit can bring its gentle touch of healing and hope to all."[10] Despite her vigor and good health, the Queen knew that in her seventh decade of service she must lay the foundation for her chosen successor, directly asking the Commonwealth leaders to approve her choice represented in the culmination of hard work, experience, and training a lifetime in the making.

Most CHOGM gatherings include several days of general sessions, issue-related meetings, state dinners, and celebratory events. After their deliberations at each summit, Commonwealth leaders have usually released an official communiqué detailing their goals and resolutions. The 2018 Commonwealth Summit proved no different, with one exception: an unprecedented statement endorsed by unanimous vote in response to a direct plea made by Her Majesty the Queen.

After two days discussing issues such as ocean conservation, cyber security, and trade between countries, Commonwealth leaders enjoyed a retreat at Windsor without their advisers or members of the Royal Family present. There the leaders voted unanimously to grant the Queen's "sincere wish" that Prince Charles be installed as Head of the Commonwealth simultaneous with his eventual accession as King. While approval for Charles as his mother's successor was never seriously in doubt, it was not guaranteed—nor is it promised for Prince William or any future monarchs.

Following the historic vote, Britain's prime minister at the time, Theresa May, announced the outcome. She began by thanking the Queen, expressing gratitude on behalf of all Commonwealth citizens "for everything Her Majesty has done and will continue to do." May emphasized the crucial role the Queen has played in the success of the Commonwealth, noting the monarch's "vision, duty and steadfast service . . . in nurturing the growth of this remarkable family of nations."[11]

May, who resigned in June 2019 amid the turmoil of Brexit, clearly enjoyed being a messenger of good news: "Today we have agreed that the next Head of the Commonwealth will be His Royal Highness Prince Charles, the Prince of Wales. His Royal Highness has been a proud supporter of the Commonwealth for more than four decades and has spoken passionately about the organization's unique diversity. It is fitting that he will one day continue the work of his mother, Her Majesty the Queen."[12]

Emphasizing the "incredible opportunity" represented by the Commonwealth to implement solutions to some of the twenty-first century's greatest problems, May concluded by paying tribute to the Queen's leadership: "You have been true to the deepest values of the Commonwealth—that the voice of the smallest member country is worth precisely as much as that of the largest; that the wealthiest and the most vulnerable stand shoulder to shoulder."[13]

Prince Charles accepted the honor and committed to serve with humility and grace. "I am deeply touched and honoured by the decision of Commonwealth Heads of State and Government that I should succeed The Queen, in due course, as Head of the Commonwealth," he said. "Meanwhile, I will continue to support Her Majesty in every possible way, in the service of our unique family of nations."[14]

While the Queen made no formal statement in response, Her Majesty's pleasure was evident the following day at a concert in honor of her ninety-second birthday at Royal Albert

Hall. Clearly, she had received the only birthday present she had requested, a gift from grateful leaders willing to place their confidence in her legacy. They knew, as so many are now aware, that their future leader, Prince Charles, has been trained by the best.

The significance of the Commonwealth's formal approval cannot be underestimated. Royal biographer Robert Hardman stressed, "It is a very big deal—a landmark in the modern royal story. It is by far the most significant step to date in the Prince's gradual evolution from Heir to the Throne to King-in-waiting. It is also a very robust validation of all that the Queen has done for this organization over the years."[15]

There have certainly been many steps along Charles's lifelong journey to the throne. Just as his mother has become the longest-reigning monarch in British history, Charles has served as heir longer than any other eventual monarch. When he becomes King, he will be the oldest sovereign ever to take the throne. These facts only underscore the lengthy, intensive preparation he has experienced.

Beginning when he was only five years old, the Queen's firstborn son has remained in the public eye as heir to the throne. In 1954 he and his sister, Princess Anne, only three at the time, set sail on the brand-new Royal Yacht, *Britannia*, for its maiden voyage in order to liaise with their parents in Malta, reuniting the Royal Family after the Queen's successful tour of the Commonwealth after her coronation. With his childhood and early adolescence focused on his education, Charles had minimal responsibility apart from family events. Nonetheless, he observed, just as his mother had done, the inner workings of relationships, tradition, and events attempting to work in harmony behind palace doors.

Although Charles was designated Prince of Wales (and Earl of Chester) when he was ten, his formal investiture did not occur until his twenty-first birthday, in 1969. In a televised ceremony held at Caernarfon Castle in northwest Wales, the Queen recognized her son and heir as an adult by allowing him to assume all rights and responsibilities inherent to the honor. The following year, Charles embraced his new title by accepting his seat in the House of Lords, where he gave his maiden speech as a Member of Parliament in 1974. He was the first royal to speak in the House of Lords since his great-great-grandfather, the son of Queen Victoria and Prince Albert, who reigned as King Edward VII.

By this time, Prince Charles was often being called on to act *in loco reginae*, the Latin phrase meaning "in place of the Queen." Following the example of his parents, he began traveling more on behalf of the Crown, both formally and informally. He had already spent months in Australia as a seventeen-year-old attending Timbertop, the Outward Bound branch of a prestigious school in Victoria. But as the newly invested Prince of Wales, His Royal Highness visited the US, along with his sister, as a guest of President Richard Nixon.

This trip would be the first of many visits that increasingly became more authoritatively royal in nature. Two such occasions particularly stand out. In 1980 Charles led a delegation to oversee the transition of Rhodesia, torn apart by a guerilla-fought civil war, into the independent nation of Zimbabwe. Then in 1997 the Queen sent Prince Charles to Hong Kong to oversee its transition as a British colony to its absorption by mainland China, labeled worldwide as the "end of the British Empire." This was also *Britannia*'s last cruise as the official Royal Yacht.

In 1976 Prince Charles founded The Prince's Trust, a charity focused on helping at-risk young people to make a successful transition into adulthood. Since then, he has gone on to establish nineteen more charitable organizations and serves as president over all of them. Collectively, they are known as The Prince's Charities, the multifaceted centerpiece of The Prince of Wales's Charitable Foundation, which describes itself as "the largest multi-cause charitable enterprise in the United Kingdom, raising over £100 million annually" and serving across "a broad range of areas including education and young people, environmental sustainability, the built environment, and responsible business."[16]

In total, Prince Charles now serves as patron of more than four hundred charities and service organizations throughout the Commonwealth. Through the steady guidance, patient training, and loving wisdom of Her Majesty the Queen, the heir to the throne has weathered his own peaks and valleys to arrive at an elevated plateau of complete preparation for the crown. He has reinvented himself in the likeness of both parents. "The old narrative—that he is either a restless royal meddler or half of the most famous marriage breakdown in history—are both well out of date as the Prince enters his eighth decade."[17]

Particularly striking is the way Prince Charles has become more overt in describing his own personal faith in recent years. Perhaps he's once again following Her Majesty's example, but now that he is in his seventies, the Prince of Wales makes his spiritual beliefs and their personal practice quite clear. Criticized over the years for appearing to espouse so-called New Age beliefs, the future King seems comfortably settled in his Christian faith, made explicitly clear both in recent interviews and his current website.

Charles describes himself and his wife, the Duchess of Cornwall, as Christians and members of the Church of England who maintain regular personal devotions. He also emphasizes their frequent meetings with church leaders and members of the Christian community across many denominations. "The Prince of Wales has also, over many years, made clear that, as a committed Christian with a strong personal faith, he believes very strongly that the world in which we live can only become a safer and more united place if we all make the effort to tolerate, accept and understand cultures, beliefs and faiths different from our own. For this reason, he has spent a lot of time encouraging dialogue and good relations between Britain's main faith communities."[18]

In other words, like mother, like son.

Without a doubt, Her Majesty Queen Elizabeth II has forever redefined the British monarchy, an institution fractured by historical complexity. Instead of simply shoring up its structure or adding an overlay of veneered nostalgia, the Queen has taken the materials given her and built a modern monarchy capable of withstanding postmodern storms of political upheaval, economic fluctuation, and social distress. That she has done it on her own terms remains a remarkable achievement. That she credits her faith in God as she follows the example of his Son, her Savior, Jesus Christ, echoes even louder.

Bridging the twentieth and twenty-first centuries, modernity and postmodernity, Her Majesty credits her personal faith in God and belief in Christ as her anchor amid the many storms, both public and private, she has endured. With humility, dignity, and a keen sense of her own humanity, Queen Elizabeth models a blend of historical tradition and entrepreneurial initiative, public service and private devotion. As a result, she has become an icon of stability, longevity, and integrity.

If, in many ways, the Queen's destiny was triggered by the abdication of her uncle, King Edward VIII, to marry the woman he loved, then there's a peculiar irony, perhaps even poetic justice, in the way Queen Elizabeth has empowered the monarchy for future generations by embracing the power of love in the lives of her children and grandchildren. This change emerges most recently in her warm acceptance of Meghan Markle, a divorced actress of multiethnic heritage, as the wife of Prince Harry and mother of their son, Master Archie. That Ms. Markle was divorced and biracial merited no consideration.

Now at the height of her popularity, Her Majesty continues to touch countless lives. Part princess and part pope, both guardian and great-grandmother, diplomat and disciple, Her Majesty the Queen is the calm that carries on, stabilizing her nation and the Commonwealth during one of the most tumultuous periods of historical change and technological advancement.

She is also a beacon of inspiration for countless admirers and an example of mature faith for millions of Christians worldwide. Above all else, she is simply a follower of Jesus who has lived faithfully and served all those entrusted to her care. "Ultimately, monarchy points beyond itself to the majesty of God," Ian Bradley has explained. "It encourages the God-given human faculties of reverence, loyalty and worship. It derives its true sanction and authority from above rather than from below."[19]

Several years ago, while hiking in Scotland, I thought I glimpsed Her Majesty the Queen. I had just rounded a hilly bend, and there she was. Like an apparition in the golden glow of a late summer afternoon, she stood several hundred yards ahead of me, a lone figure on a promontory, taking in the rugged beauty of the Highlands. I remember thinking, *Is it possible? Could it be?*

After all, I probably was within a mile or two of the edge of her Balmoral estate. For all I knew, I might have been *on* her property since the Cairngorms National Park where I began my trek also contains the fifty thousand acres of her family's property. Although it was late July, I knew the Queen retreated to Balmoral every year, usually not until August, for summer holiday.

Dressed in khaki pants and an old Barbour jacket, wearing large dark sunglasses and a plaid scarf covering her head, the woman appeared like a windblown statue, a bit disheveled but solid and regal nonetheless. Something about her stance conveyed someone advanced in age yet still fit. I slowed my pace and worried about what to do. Although my trail would not take me past her, it did approach the place where she stood. What would I say if it really was the Queen? It seemed surreal to even consider meeting her here in the middle of nowhere.

Then hearing me or seeing movement from the corner of her eye, she turned and automatically brought her hand up to shield her eyes for a better look. I raised my hand in a friendly wave, and for a brief moment, I thought she appeared angry or cross with me for interrupting her solitude. But then she raised her hand to return my gesture and offered the hint of a smile. The wind kicked up, so I gave up my thought of calling out to her. And what would I say anyway, other than "hello"?

I picked up my pace again and decided to keep going.

When she realized I was going to continue on my hike without approaching her, she gave a little nod and her face blossomed into a full smile before she turned her back to me again. As she crossed her arms and returned to being part of the landscape, I sensed relief, as if she could resume her meditation, an escape from whatever responsibilities might await in her other life.

I thought about that encounter for the rest of my ramble that day, and many times since. Then as now, my logical brain continues to tell me that it's highly unlikely that this woman was Her Majesty. Still . . . my heart holds on to the possibility.

Throughout my life, the more I've learned about her, the more I have admired the Queen's ability to accomplish an impossible job. My appreciation and admiration for her has only grown while researching and writing this book. Her poise, grace, and quiet strength continue to inspire me, along with countless others. Her faith, in both word and deed, reminds us to keep going, to take another step each day in fulfilling the spiritual journey on which we are all pilgrims. To show kindness and respect to all those we meet. To serve everyone from the bounty of blessings we've been given.

Elizabeth Alexandra Mary Windsor. Lilibet. Princess. Her Royal Highness. Queen Elizabeth II, by the Grace of God, the Queen of Great Britain and Head of the Commonwealth, Her Other Realms, and Territories. Defender of the Faith. Her Majesty. Daughter, sister, wife, mother, grandmother, and great-grandmother. No matter her title or role, Queen Elizabeth II reflects the love of the King she serves.

May she continue to reign with strength, stamina, and the servant's heart that has become her hallmark. Whether offered as national anthem or fervent prayer, may all we who have been blessed by her example join the chorus: God save the Queen!

ACKNOWLEDGMENTS

*T*his book proved to be one of the most challenging as well as fulfilling of my career. Writing a book, as with many creative endeavors, requires long periods of isolation along with strategic intervals of support, encouragement, and collaboration. The Crown employs more than a thousand people to keep the Queen's office, royal residences, and properties in the best working order for Her Majesty and the Royal Family. While the number of people who have helped me while writing this book is not as large, their contributions are no less significant.

I'm sincerely grateful to the subject of this book, Her Majesty Queen Elizabeth II, for her example of strength, humility, compassion, and service not only as the longest-reigning monarch in British history but foremost as a devoted follower of Jesus Christ in word and deed. The more I learned about her over the course of my research, the more I appreciated the mettle of her character, the sacrifice of her service, and the kindness of her spirit. Thank you, Your Majesty, for inspiring so many of us to keep the faith.

My hearty thanks to the entire team—editorial, marketing, sales—at Zondervan and HarperCollins Christian Publishing. I especially appreciate the contributions of Bridgette Brooks, Keith Finnegan, Kim Tanner, Dale Williams, and all the team members who played a part in making this book come to life.

Carolyn McCready, my editor, proved herself more than worthy of a royal title! Thank you, Lady Carolyn, for your insight, wisdom, encouragement, and support. Your patience, understanding, and belief in me as a writer made an enormous difference and helped me overcome numerous unexpected obstacles. You have made this a much better book, and I'm so grateful to have you as my editor and as my friend.

I'm indebted to Lori Vanden Bosch for her editorial expertise as well. Lori, your fascination with all things Royal rivals my own, which only enhanced your contribution. Thank you for your encouragement of my writing, your validation of my primary focus, and your clarifications in the text, all of which made this a better book. You too deserve a royal title!

While I'm handing out royal titles, I must add my publisher and good friend, David Morris, to the list. David, you are a champion of good books and quality writing, and you always follow through. Thank you for believing in this book from the first time I mentioned it. Your support, encouragement, and friendship liberate me to be a better writer and a better man. And I would be remiss without thanking your wife, Lisa, as well. Lisa, I speak for my entire family in expressing gratitude for your kindness and hospitality.

So many people helped me on the other side of the pond.

Foremost, I'm especially grateful for Andy Pratt, who saw the potential for this book from its inception. Thank you, Andy, for sharing your knowledge, wisdom, insight, and opinions on so many aspects of British history, culture, and lifestyle. I appreciate your willingness to serve as host, tour guide, chauffeur, historian, spiritual director, and tutor. You are a kindred spirit and a cherished friend. My thanks to your lovely wife, Heather, as well for her kindness, hospitality, assistance, and insight. You are both the best of Britain and beyond!

In the UK my thanks also go out to Gareth Russell for his advice, suggestions, and wisdom. Gareth, this book proved a great reason to reconnect, and your input proved invaluable. Cheers, mate!

My thanks to Gemma, Sean, Bridget, Sheila, Yamar and Kimmy, Judy, Rami, and many others in the UK who willingly shared their thoughts, feelings, and opinions about Her Majesty the Queen. I'm also indebted to staff members at the British Library, Westminster Abbey, the British Museum, Windsor Castle, the Victoria and Albert Museum, and Buckingham Palace for their kind assistance.

Thank you, South Cumberland Celtic Voyagers, for your prayers, support, friendship, and encouragement during the writing of this book. Our meetings at St. Mary's Sewanee this past year have been life giving. I'm blessed to be on the journey with you!

Ron Winfree, you remain an anchor of strength, support, and stability—thank you, dear friend. Jim McClanahan, how wonderful to reconnect now that we're in the same state again! Thanks to you and your friend Milton Winter for reading early drafts and providing constructive feedback and encouragement.

To Kevin Kelling and Justin Reed, the First and Second Dukes of Dickel, respectively, I'm forever grateful. Thank you for cheering me on and championing my writing. I can't wait for your next visit to the Lodge!

Tony Laurie, you claimed to know I'd become a writer when I won that essay contest back in seventh grade. How wonderful to reconnect so many years later and to see that your prophecy has come true! Thank you for your friendship, brotherhood, and generosity.

I appreciate the support of my brother, Barry Tawwater, and his wife, Rhonda. Thank you for believing in what I do. It's great to live only a few miles away and see you both more often.

This book is dedicated to my mother, Norma Delffs, for teaching me that courage, character, and conviction are not reserved for royalty. Thank you, Mama, for all you've done to encourage my writing. I love you.

My children continue to amaze me as they discover their own paths on this journey. Mecie, Annie, and Jacob—you are each doing the hard work of adulting, and you're making your parents so proud! Thank you each for continuing to believe in me and what I'm called to do. I love you more than I can express.

Dotti, thank you for always treating me like a prince, especially on days when I feel like a pauper. You said you've never seen me work harder on a book than this one. I'm so grateful for the countless ways you kept me going and helped me push through all the obstacles. I couldn't do this without you. You're the one and only queen of my heart.

NOTES

Chapter 1: Duty and Desire

1. Harry Farley, "Queen Attends Scripture Union's 150th Anniversary," *Christian Today* (December 6, 2017): https://www.christiantoday .com/article/queen-attends-scripture-unions-150th-anniversary -service/120706.htm.

2. Joe Moran, "Why Elizabeth II's 1953 Coronation Is the Day that Changed Television," *RadioTimes* (June 2, 2013): https://www.radio times.com/news/2013–06–02/why-elizabeth-iis-1953-coronation-is-the -day-that-changed-television/.

3. Robert Lacey, *The Crown* (New York: Crown Archetype, 2017), 120.

4. Queen Elizabeth II, "Christmas Broadcast 1952" (published December 25, 1952): https://www.royal.uk/queens-first-christmas-broadcast-1952.

5. Hannah Furness, "Secrets of the Oil Used to Anoint the Queen at Coronation," *Telegraph* (January 14, 2018): https://www.telegraph.co.uk/ news/2018/01/14/secrets-oil-used-anoint-queen-coronation/.

6. Queen Elizabeth II, "The Queen's Coronation Oath, 1953" (published June 2, 1953): https://www.royal.uk/coronation-oath-2-june-1953.

7. Queen Elizabeth II, "A Speech by the Queen on Her Twenty-First Birthday, 1947" (published April 21, 1947): https://www.royal.uk/21st -birthday-speech-21-april-1947.

8. Joseph Lelyveld, "1936 Secret Is Out: Doctor Sped George V's Death," *New York Times* (November 28, 1986): https://www.nytimes.com/1986/ 11/28/world/1936-secret-is-out-doctor-sped-george-v-s-death.html.

9. Mike Priestley, "Not-So-Blunt Words that Stopped Coronation," *Telegraph & Argus* (December 1, 2006): https://www.thetelegraph andargus.co.uk/news/1053791.not-so-blunt-words-that-stopped -coronation/.

Chapter 2: Commitment and Conviction

1. William Shawcross, *Queen and Country* (Toronto: McClelland & Stewart, 2002), xx.
2. David Dilks, "The Queen and Mr. Churchill," address to the Royal Society of St. George, City of London Branch (February 6, 2007), published in *Finest Hour* 135 (summer 2007): https://winstonchurchill.org/publications/finest-hour/finest-hour-135/the-queen-and-mr-churchill/.
3. Ibid.
4. Winston Churchill, *Stemming the Tide* (London: Cassell, 1953), 1128.
5. Robert Lacey, *The Crown* (New York: Crown Archetype, 2017), 183.
6. Ibid., 184.
7. Robert Blake, "The Queen and the Constitution," in *The Queen, A Penguin Special* (London: Penguin, 1977), 14.
8. Ibid.
9. Lacey, *The Crown*, 115.
10. Francesca Specter, "Princess Margaret's Shock Three Words to Elizabeth as She Found Out She'd Be Ruler," *Express* (February 7, 2018): https://www.express.co.uk/life-style/life/915391/queen-elizabeth-princess-margaret-shock-three-words.
11. Ian Bradley, *God Save the Queen: The Spiritual Heart of the Monarchy* (London: Continuum, 2012), 119.
12. https://hollandparkbenefice.org/history-st-john-the-baptist-holland-road.

Chapter 3: Service and Sacrifice

1. Queen Elizabeth II, "A Speech by the Queen at Lambeth Palace, 2012" (published February 15, 2012): https://www.royal.uk/queens-speech-lambeth-palace-15-february-2012.
2. Lauren Paxman, "Cardinal Error! Queen's Papal Red Clashes with Archbishop's Purple for Event at Lambeth Palace," *Daily Mail* (February 15, 2012): https://www.dailymail.co.uk/femail/article-2101518/Queen-Elizabeth-clashes-Archbishop-Canterbury-Lambeth-Palace-event.html.
3. Sally Bedell Smith, *Elizabeth the Queen* (New York: Random House, 2011), 544–45.
4. "Tributes to Queen Mother and Princess Margaret at Windsor Memorial," *BBC News* (March 30, 2012): https://www.bbc.com/news/uk-england-berkshire-17566981.
5. Ibid.
6. Bedell Smith, *Elizabeth the Queen*, 545.
7. "The King's Speech: The Real Story," *Telegraph* (January 5, 2011): https://www.telegraph.co.uk/films/0/kings-speech-real-story/.
8. Ibid.
9. Sally Mitchell, Daily Life in Victorian England (Westport, CT: Greenwood, 2008), 5.

10. Walter Walsh, *The Religious Life of Queen Victoria* (London: Swan Sonnenschein, 1902), 184.
11. Frank Prochaska, *Royal Bounty: The Making of a Welfare Monarchy* (New Haven, CT: Yale University Press, 1995), 80.
12. Harshan Kumarasingham, "The Queen's Favourites," *The World Today* (April–May 2018): 28, https://www.chathamhouse.org/system/files/publications/twt/The%20Queen%E2%80%99s%20favourite%20club%20H%20Kumarasingham_0.pdf.
13. Ibid.
14. Ibid., 30.
15. Ibid., 30.
16. Queen Elizabeth II, "A Speech by the Queen to Parliament on Her Silver Jubilee" (published May 4, 1977): https://www.royal.uk/silver-jubilee-address-parliament-4-may-1977.
17. Kumarasingham, "The Queen's Favourites," 31.
18. Robert Hardman, *Queen of the World* (New York: Pegasus, 2019), 381.
19. Queen Elizabeth II, "Christmas Broadcast 1983" (published December 25, 1983): https://www.royal.uk/christmas-broadcast-1983.
20. Hardman, *Queen of the World*, 382.
21. Kumarasingham, "The Queen's Favourites," 31.

Chapter 4: Conviction and Compromise

1. Robert Lacey, *The Crown* (New York: Crown Archetype, 2017), 149.
2. John Grigg, "The Monarch Today," *National and English Review* (August 1957): 61–67.
3. Sally Bedell Smith, *Elizabeth the Queen* (New York: Random House, 2011), 129.
4. Ibid., 130.
5. Malcolm Muggeridge, "Does England Really Need a Queen?," *Saturday Evening Post* (October 19, 1957): 14.
6. Ibid.
7. Caroline Hallemann, "How Lord Altrincham Changed the Monarchy Forever," *Town and Country* (December 8, 2017): https://www.townandcountrymag.com/society/tradition/a14273687/lord-altrincham-john-grigg-role-british-history/.
8. Bedell Smith, *Elizabeth the Queen*, 131.
9. Ibid., 138.
10. Queen Elizabeth II, "Christmas Broadcast 1957" (published December 25, 1957): https://www.royal.uk/christmas-broadcast-1957.
11. Ibid.

Chapter 5: Time and Tide

1. Queen Elizabeth II, "Reply to the Loyal Addresses by Both Houses

of Parliament" (April 30, 2002): https://www.royal.uk/reply-loyal
-addresses-both-houses-parliament-30-april-2002.

2. Tony Blair, *A Journey: My Political Life* (New York: Knopf, 2010), 16.

3. Warren Hoge, "British Leave Hong Kong in Sour Kind of Grandeur,"
New York Times (March 27, 1997): https://www.nytimes.com/1997/03/
27/world/british-leave-hong-kong-in-sour-kind-of-grandeur.html.

4. The Royal Yacht *Britannia*: Edinburgh, https://www.royalyachtbritannia
.co.uk/about/history/.

5. William Kuhn, *Mrs. Queen Takes the Train* (New York: HarperCollins,
2012), 284.

6. https://www.royalyachtbritannia.co.uk/about/royal-residence/
decommission/.

7. Ben Pimlott, *The Queen: A Biography of Elizabeth II* (New York: John
Wiley & Sons, 1996), 548.

8. Ibid., 574.

9. Queen Elizabeth II, "A Speech by the Queen on the 40th Anniversary
of Her Succession (Annus Horribilis Speech)" (published November 24,
1992): https://www.royal.uk/annus-horribilis-speech.

10. Queen Elizabeth II, "Christmas Broadcast 1992" (published
December 25, 1992): https://www.royal.uk/christmas-broadcast-1992.

11. Queen Elizabeth II, "Christmas Broadcast 2002" (published
December 25, 2002): https://www.royal.uk/christmas-broadcast-2002.

Chapter 6: Grace and Grit

1. Jennifer Rosenberg, "Intruder Enters Queen Elizabeth's Bedroom,"
ThoughtCo. (updated March 8, 2019): https://www.thoughtco.com/
intruder-enters-queen-elizabeths-bedroom-1779399.

2. Emily Dugan, "Michael Fagan: Her Nightie Was One of Those Liberty
Prints, Down to Her Knees," *Independent* (February 19, 2012): https://
www.independent.co.uk/news/people/profiles/michael-fagan-her
-nightie-was-one-of-those-liberty-prints-down-to-her-knees-7179547.
html.

3. Ibid.

4. "Text of Scotland Yard's Report on July 9 Intrusion into Buckingham
Palace," *New York Times* (July 22, 1982): https://www.nytimes.com/
1982/07/22/world/text-of-scotland-yard-s-report-on-july-9-intrusion
-into-buckingham-palace.html.

5. Sally Bedell Smith, *Elizabeth the Queen* (New York: Random House,
2011), 301.

6. "Elizabeth at 90: A Family Tribute," BBC, 2016.

7. Bedell Smith, *Elizabeth the Queen*, 301.

8. Steven Rattner, "British Police Investigating Blast at Oil Plant During
Queen's Visit," *New York Times* (May 13, 1981): https://www.nytimes

.com/1981/05/13/world/british-police-investigating-blast-at-oil-plant
-during-queen-s-visit.html.

9. Michael Rosenwald, "Beloved Lord Mountbatten Was Killed by
Terrorists; Now He's a Royal Baby's Namesake," *Washington Post*
(April 28, 2018): https://www.washingtonpost.com/news/retropolis/
wp/2018/04/28/beloved-lord-mountbatten-was-killed-by-terrorists-now
-hes-a-royal-babys-namesake/?utm_term=.417fcbf90b8f.

10. Kenzie Bryant, "An Assassination Attempt on Queen Elizabeth Was
Covered Up by New Zealand Officials for Thirty Years," *Vanity Fair*
(March 1, 2018): https://www.vanityfair.com/style/2018/03/queen
-elizabeth-ii-assassination-attempt-new-zealand.

11. Bedell Smith, *Elizabeth the Queen*, 301.

12. Julie Miller, "*The Crown*: What Really Happened When Queen
Elizabeth Met John and Jackie Kennedy," *Vanity Fair* (December 8,
2017): https://www.vanityfair.com/hollywood/2017/12/queen-elizabeth
-jackie-kennedy-the-crown-netflix.

Chapter 7: Example and Exemplar

1. Warren Hoge, "Design Notebook: 'Honey, They Fixed Up the Castle!',"
New York Times (November 20, 1997): https://www.nytimes.com
/1997/11/20/garden/design-notebook-honey-they-fixed-up-the-castle
.html.

2. Sally Bedell Smith, *Elizabeth the Queen* (New York: Random House,
2011), 412.

3. Catherine Armecin, "Royal Family Documentary Shows People's
Stories of Meeting Queen, Princess Diana," *International Business Times*
(August 19, 2018): https://www.ibtimes.com/royal-family-documentary
-shows-peoples-stories-meeting-queen-princess-diana-2709622.

4. Ben Pimlott, *The Queen* (New York: John Wiley & Sons, 1996), 75.

5. Bedell Smith, *Elizabeth the Queen*, 68.

6. Ibid., 293.

7. Ibid., 294.

8. Simon Freeman, "Queen Dismayed by 'Uncaring' Thatcher," *Sunday
Times* (July 20, 1986): 1.

9. Molly West, "The Only Time Princess Margaret Saw the Queen Cry,"
Woman & Home (March 28, 2018): https://www.womanandhome.com/
life/royal-news/princess-margaret-queen-cry-244196/.

10. Michael Billington, "*The Audience*: Review," *The Guardian* (March 5,
2013): https://www.theguardian.com/stage/2013/mar/05/the-audience
-review-helen-mirren.

11. Queen Elizabeth II, "Christmas Broadcast 1980" (published
December 25, 1980): https://www.royal.uk/christmas-broadcast-1980.

12. Ibid.

Chapter 8: Comfort and Compassion

1. David Nott, *War Doctor: Surgery on the Front Line* (London: Picador, 2019), 289.
2. "Surgeon David Nott Recalls How Queen's Corgis Helped Him," BBC News (June 5, 2016): https://www.bbc.com/news/uk-36455715.
3. Nott, *War Doctor*, 289.
4. "Surgeon David Nott Recalls," BBC News.
5. "The Queen Attends a Service at the Royal Army Chaplains' Department" (published February 22, 2019): https://www.royal.uk/queen-attends-service-royal-army-chaplains'-department.
6. "Remembrance Day" (accessed May 20, 2019): https://www.royal.uk/remembrance-day.
7. Ian Bradley, *God Save the Queen: The Spiritual Heart of the Monarchy* (London: Continuum, 2012), 207.
8. Robert Lacey, *Monarch: The Life and Reign of Elizabeth II* (New York: Free Press, 2002), 378–79.
9. Queen Elizabeth II, "Tribute to Princess Diana on the Eve of Her Funeral" (eulogy, Buckingham Palace, London, September 9, 1997), https://americanrhetoric.com/speeches/queenelizabethprincessdianaeulogy.htm.
10. Queen Elizabeth II, "Queen's Message to New York" (read by the British ambassador to Washington, Sir Christopher Meyer, at the prayer service in St. Thomas Church, New York City, September 21, 2001): https://www.theguardian.com/world/2001/sep/21/september11.usa12.
11. Ibid.
12. Daniel Bates, "'Worst Thing I've Ever Seen': Queen Tells Widow of Her Horror on 9/11 as She Visits Ground Zero," *Daily Mail* (July 7, 2010): https://www.dailymail.co.uk/news/article-1292594/Queen-tells-widow-horror-9-11-visits-Ground-Zero.html.
13. Queen Elizabeth II, "A Message from the Queen Following the Fire at Grenfell Tower Yesterday" (published June 15, 2017): https://www.royal.uk/message-queen-following-fire-grenfell-tower-yesterday.
14. Alan Cowell, "I Can't Give You Anything But Love, She Said. And Did," *New York Times* (April 19, 2006): https://www.nytimes.com/2006/04/19/world/europe/19queen.html.
15. Queen Elizabeth II, "Christmas Broadcast 2000" (published December 25, 2000): https://www.royal.uk/christmas-broadcast-2000.

Chapter 9: Wit and Wisdom

1. Chilli Brener, *What the Queen Said to Me* (London: Unicorn, 2017), 20.
2. Ibid.
3. Ibid.
4. Ibid., 22–23.

5. Karen Dolby, *The Wicked Wit of Queen Elizabeth II* (London: Michael O'Mara, 2015), 45.
6. Robert Pierre, "Alice Frazier, at 81; Southerner Hugged Queen Elizabeth II," *Boston Globe* (March 20, 2005): http://archive.boston.com/news/globe/obituaries/articles/2005/03/20/alice_frazier_at_81_southerner_hugged_queen_elizabeth_ii/.
7. Dolby, *The Wicked Wit*, 47.
8. Sally Bedell Smith, *Elizabeth the Queen* (New York: Random House, 2011), 311.
9. Dolby, *The Wicked Wit*, 9.
10. "Queen Teases Bush Over Verbal Gaffe," *The Guardian* (May 9, 2007): https://www.theguardian.com/world/2007/may/09/usa.monarchy.
11. Ibid.
12. Bedell Smith, *Elizabeth the Queen*, 312.
13. Ibid., 313.
14. William Shawcross, *The Servant Queen and the King She Serves* (Swindon, UK: Bible Society, 2016), 27.
15. Dolby, *The Wicked Wit*, 35.
16. Paul Harris, "The Moment the Queen Photobombed the BBC: Monarch Makes a Surprise Appearance on Live TV News Bulletin," *Daily Mail* (June 8, 2013): https://www.dailymail.co.uk/news/article-2337835/The-moment-Queen-photobombed-BBC-Monarch-makes-surprise-appearance-live-TV-news-bulletin.html.
17. Dolby, *The Wicked Wit*, 37.
18. Caroline Halleman, "The True Story of Queen Elizabeth's Friendship with Reverend Billy Graham," *Town and Country* (February 21, 2018): https://www.townandcountrymag.com/leisure/arts-and-culture/a14107629/queen-elizabeth-billy-graham-friendship/.
19. Shawcross, *The Servant Queen*, 16–17.
20. "Elizabeth II Quotes," ThinkExist.com, http://thinkexist.com/quotation/to-what-greater-inspiration-and-counsel-can-we/348780.html.
21. Queen Elizabeth II, "Christmas Broadcast 2016" (published December 25, 2016): https://www.royal.uk/christmas-broadcast-2016.
22. "Billy Graham Reflects on His Friendship with Queen Elizabeth II," Billy Graham Evangelistic Association (December 11, 2017): https://billygraham.org/story/billy-graham-and-the-queen/.
23. Halleman, "The True Story of Queen Elizabeth's Friendship with Reverend Billy Graham."
24. Billy Graham Evangelistic Association, "Billy Graham Reflects on His Friendship with Queen Elizabeth II."
25. Ibid.
26. Ibid.

27. Ibid.
28. Shawcross, *The Servant Queen*, 1.

Chapter 10: Mystery and Majesty

1. Hayley Dixon and Claire Carter, "Portrait of the Queen Sprayed with Paint in Westminster Abbey," *Telegraph* (June 13, 2013): https://www.telegraph.co.uk/news/uknews/queen-elizabeth-II/10118395/Portrait-of-the-Queen-sprayed-with-paint-in-Westminster-Abbey.html.

2. Ibid.

3. Ibid.

4. "Queen's Portrait Defaced with Spray Paint in Westminster Abbey," BBC News (June 13, 2103): https://www.bbc.com/news/uk-22892297.

5. Ibid.

6. "First Public Display in London for Diamond Jubilee Portrait of The Queen," Westminster Abbey (May 19, 2013): https://www.westminster-abbey.org/abbey-news/first-public-display-in-london-for-diamond-jubilee-portrait-of-the-queen#i12334.

7. William Shawcross, *The Servant Queen and the King She Serves: A Tribute for Her Majesty's 90th Birthday* (Swindon, UK: Bible Society, 2016), 6.

8. Laura Smith-Spark, "Britain's Queen Hopes Prince Charles Will 'One Day' Lead Commonwealth," BBC News (April 19, 2018): https://www.cnn.com/2018/04/19/europe/queen-prince-charles-commonwealth-meeting-intl/index.html.

9. "Commonwealth Meeting: Queen Hopes Prince Charles Will Succeed Her," BBC News (April 19, 2018): https://www.bbc.com/news/uk-politics-43820328.

10. Ibid.

11. Hannah Furness, "Prince Charles 'Deeply Touched' to Be Confirmed as Queen's Head of the Commonwealth Successor," *Telegraph* (April 20, 2018): https://www.telegraph.co.uk/news/2018/04/20/prince-charles-confirmed-successor-queen-next-head-commonwealth/.

12. Ibid.

13. Ibid.

14. Ibid.

15. Robert Hardman, *Queen of the World* (New York: Pegasus, 2019), 465.

16. "The Prince of Wales's Charities," Prince of Wales (accessed May 29, 2019): https://www.princeofwales.gov.uk/prince-waless-charities.

17. Hardman, *Queen of the World*, 467.

18. "Do the Prince and the Duchess Attend Church?", Prince of Wales (accessed May 29, 2019): https://www.princeofwales.gov.uk/do-prince-and-duchess-attend-church.

19. Ian Bradley, *God Save the Queen: The Spiritual Heart of the Monarchy* (London: Continuum, 2012), 275.